Praise for
Assassination Vacation

"Part history lesson, part hilarious travelogue, the charmingly obsessed Vowell's stories cheerfully highlight the oft-appalling ways in which popular culture has spun these politically based murders into tragitainment. . . . With Sarah Vowell at the wheel, *Assassination Vacation* is a far-out trip into America's storied past. I call shotgun."

—Elissa Schappell, *Vanity Fair*

"This is a book like no other, a serious and interesting romp through loopholes of time and American political violence. Vowell likes to explode myths and reveal hypocrisy wherever she finds it. . . . Vowell is an American original. . . . She is somehow simultaneously patriot and rebel, cynic and dreamer, and an aching secularist in search of a higher ground. Her book—part memoir, part meditation, and part road trip—will attract readers who are still unafraid of having many of their assumptions challenged."

—Elaine Margolin, *The Atlanta Journal-Constitution*

"Vowell takes as her province the innumerable eccentric ways that people manage to squeeze personal and civic meaning out of a world framed by pop culture. . . . Her wit makes these stories funny, of course, but so do her curiosity and ear for vernacular, which yield further revelation and insight."

—*The Washington Post*

"A winking rumination on the murders of Abraham Lincoln, James Garfield, and William McKinley."

—*Entertainment Weekly*

"A funny-grim travelogue . . ."

—John Mark Eberhart, *The Kansas City Star*

"Darkly comic and fascinating miscellany about presidential assassinations."

—Elizabeth Barr, *Buffalo News*

"*Assassination Vacation* is a beguiling mixture of memoir, history, and humor. . . . Despite the grimness of the topic, *Assassination Vacation* is a fresh, fun read from a talented writer."

—John Keenan, *Omaha World-Herald*

"Adventure, intrigue, and laughs . . . [a] witty book. . . . Vowell takes readers to various historic locations and explains in her inimitable way why each is relevant to one of the assassinations."

—Amy Carlson Gustafson, *Saint Paul Pioneer Press* (Minnesota)

"One of the things that makes *Assassination Vacation* so rewarding is that it's a book in love with history."

—*The Virginian-Pilot* (Norfolk, VA)

"It is her gift for details that gives life to historical figures and adds a new dimension to the textbook topic of presidential assassinations."

—Siri Agrell, *National Post* (Toronto)

"Funny and perceptive. . . . The book is a hoot, entertaining, bemused, even educational. Vowell deeply loves American history, especially its strange byways and unexpected connections; but never once, while reading this, will it feel like you'll be tested after class. Instead, more than likely, you will annoy your spouse by wanting to read the best parts out loud. The book's a combo plate of quirky observation and droll insights, a dish Vowell consistently serves. . . . These commentaries are the thoughtful and thought-provoking musings of a genuine patriot—one who loves her country even if its politics disappoint her."

—Adam Woog, *The Seattle Times*

"Buy it now. . . . Vowell's writing combines historical fact, pop references, and her own wiseacre observations, a mix that can astound you and make you laugh out loud, and sometimes both at once."

—Liz Braun, *Toronto Sun*

"Vowell reclaims her quirky 'This American Life' appeal with this funny, off-kilter book about presidential assassinations. You'll never think about President James A. Garfield the same way again."

—*Wisconsin State Journal* (Madison)

"*Assassination Vacation* . . . blends travelogue; weird-but-true history lessons; and [Vowell's] own quirky, hilarious, and downright profound thoughts on the American character."

—*Wisconsin State Journal* (Madison)

"In *Assassination Vacation,* Vowell offers a take on history that is less footnoted, less grainy-footage History Channel type stuff, more *Laugh-In* in Technicolor. . . . History as you've never listened to it."

—*Newsday*

"Vowell could make a trip to the DMV interesting. Delighting in the ironies and oddities of America's past, she succeeds by telling history through her own skewed filter. . . . Part travelogue, part history text, and part memoir, *Assassination Vacation* is more fun than it has any right to be—a bizarre road trip into some of the most searing moments of the nation's past with one of our most amusing storytellers at the wheel."

—*The Baltimore Sun*

"Illuminating, often insightful, and always interesting."

—*Rocky Mountain News*

"Equal parts textbook, guidebook, and memoir, *Assassination Vacation* takes readers on an informative and (where appropriate) hilarious tour of some of the darkest moments in our nation's history."

—*The Star-Ledger* (Newark, NJ)

"Sarah Vowell . . . guides us to places connected to politicians who met a bloody end. Sound gruesome? With Vowell, such a journey is hilarious, informative, and about as quirky as it gets."

—Margo Hammond, *St. Petersburg Times*

"[Vowell's] aim is to make us see the past in new ways. And she succeeds: In Vowell's hands a presidential nonentity like Garfield . . . gains depth and dimension. . . . Any writer who can put James A. Garfield and Lou Reed in the same sentence leaves me in slack-jawed awe."

—Charles Matthews, *San Jose Mercury News*

"Cutting through cant with a satirical scalpel, she is the history teacher we all wanted in school: whip-smart, hilariously self-deprecating, and gifted with the power to make the invisible appear vividly before our eyes."

—*The Miami Herald*

"Vowell's somewhat macabre enthusiasm for her subject matter bubbles over onto every page of [*Assassination Vacation*], as she unearths fascinating and eerie details about the assassinations and entertainingly recounts her trips to tourist spots like Lincoln's tomb. Reading the book is like having lunch with a very smart, funny friend who wants to talk about a subject that you couldn't care less about. And by the end of the lunch, you're begging her for a suggested reading list."

—*The Capital Times* (Madison, WI)

"*Assassination Vacation* . . . reads like Jack Kerouac's *On the Road*, minus the drugs and run-on sentences. Peripatetic, distinctly American, and always enthusiastic, it recounts journeys Vowell made to satisfy her curiosities about the legacies of assassinated presidents. . . . Vowell is the perfect tour guide to our country's bloody past. She approaches her subject with a raconteur's wit and the unguarded passion of a fan."

—*Time Out New York*

"Vowell . . . burrows into the past with an academic's zeal, making seemingly absurd connections that have their own logic and witty truths. . . . She travels with a patriot's devotion and an observer's eye for the priceless."

—New York *Daily News*

"Hilarious . . . [Vowell] is flat-out funny. . . . She is a master of the bon mot, and the associations she makes compel the reader to call up their literary friends and share the insights."

—*The News Tribune* (Tacoma, WA)

Also by **SARAH VOWELL**

The Partly Cloudy Patriot
Take the Cannoli: Stories from the New World
Radio On: A Listener's Diary

ASSASSINATION VACATION

SARAH VOWELL

SIMON & SCHUSTER PAPERBACKS

new york   london   toronto   sydney

SIMON & SCHUSTER PAPERBACKS
Rockefeller Center
1230 Avenue of the Americas
New York, NY 10020

First Simon & Schuster paperback edition 2006
SIMON & SCHUSTER PAPERBACKS and colophon are registered trademarks
of Simon & Schuster, Inc.

For information regarding special discounts for bulk purchases,
please contact Simon & Schuster Special Sales at 1-800-456-6798
or business@simonandschuster.com

Illustrations by Marcel Dzama
Designed by Jeanette Olender

Manufactured in the United States of America

20 19 18 17 16 15 14 13 12 11

The Library of Congress has catalogued the hardcover edition as follows:
Vowell, Sarah.
Assassination vacation / Sarah Vowell.
p. cm.
1. Presidents—United States—Assassination. 2. Presidents—United
States—Biography. 3. Presidents—Homes and haunts—United States.
4. Assassins—United States—Biography. 5. Assassins—Homes and
haunts—United States. 6. Historic sites—United States.
7. United States—History, local. 8. United States—Description
and travel. 9. Vowell, Sarah—Travel—United States. I. Title.
E176.1.V89 2005   973'.09'9—dc22
[B]   2004059134

ISBN 13: 978-0-7432-6003-9
ISBN 10:   0-7432-6003-1
ISBN 13: 978-0-7432-6004-6 (Pbk)
ISBN 10:   0-7432-6004-X (Pbk)

In memory of Carlile Vowell (1904–1995)

Grandfather, principal, history teacher, Muskogee County commissioner, wiseacre, and Democrat. What I wouldn't give to hear him cuss that a book about three Republicans has been dedicated in his name.

In the Middle Ages, relics spawned a continentwide craze. Devotees packed their bags and streamed out of towns and villages, thronging the pilgrimage trails. For most, a journey to see the relic of St. Thomas or St. James offered the only valid excuse for leaving home.

ANNELI RUFUS *Magnificent Corpses*

"The real Lincoln exists in my mind," Pris said.

I was astonished. "You don't believe that. What do you mean by saying that? You mean you have the *idea* in your mind."

She cocked her head on one side and eyed me. "No, Louis. I really have Lincoln in my mind. And I've been working night after night to transfer him out of my mind, back into the outside world."

PHILIP K. DICK *We Can Build You*

That's what writing is. You're keeping people alive in your head.

CARL REINER

PREFACE

One night last summer, all the killers in my head assembled on a stage in Massachusetts to sing show tunes. There they were—John Wilkes Booth, Charles Guiteau, Leon Czolgosz—in tune and in the flesh. The men who murdered Presidents Lincoln, Garfield, and McKinley were elbow to elbow with Lee Harvey Oswald and the klutzy girls who botched their hits on klutzy Gerald Ford, harmonizing on a toe-tapper called "Everybody's Got the Right to Be Happy," a song I cheerfully hummed walking back to the bed-and-breakfast where I was staying.

Not that I came all the way from New York City just to enjoy a chorus line of presidential assassins. Mostly, I came to the Berkshires because of the man who brought one of those presidents back to life. I was there to visit Chesterwood, the house and studio once belonging to Daniel Chester French, the artist responsible for the Abraham Lincoln sculpture in the Lincoln Memorial. A nauseating four-hour bus ride from the Port Authority terminal just to see the room where some patriotic chiseler came up with a marble statue? For some reason, none of my friends wanted to come with.

Because I had to stay overnight and this being New England, the only place to stay was a bed-and-breakfast. It was a lovely old country mansion operated by amiable people. That said, I am not a bed-and-breakfast person.

I understand why other people would want to stay in B&Bs. They're pretty. They're personal. They're "quaint," a polite way of saying "no TV." They are "romantic," i.e., every object large enough for a flower to be printed on it is going to have a flower printed on it. They're "cozy," meaning that a guest has to keep her belongings on the floor because every conceivable flat surface is covered in knickknacks, except for the one knickknack she longs for, a remote control.

The real reason bed-and-breakfasts make me nervous is breakfast. As if it's not queasy enough to stay in a stranger's home and sleep in a bed bedecked with nineteen pillows. In the morning, the usually cornflake-consuming, wheat-intolerant guest is served floury baked goods on plates so fancy any normal person would keep them locked in the china cabinet even if Queen Victoria herself rose from the dead and showed up for tea. The guest, normally a silent morning reader of newspapers, is expected to chat with the other strangers staying in the strangers' home.

At my Berkshires bed-and-breakfast, I am seated at a table with one middle-aged Englishman and an elderly couple from Greenwich, Connecticut. The three of them make small talk about golf, the weather, and the room's chandeliers, one of which, apparently, is Venetian. I cannot think of a thing to say to these people. Seated at the head of the table, I am the black hole of breakfast, a silent void of gloom sucking the sunshine out of their neighborly New England day. But that is not the kind of girl my mother raised me to be. I consider asking the Connecticut couple if they had ever run into Jack Paar, who I heard had retired near where they live, but I look like I was born after Paar quit hosting *The Tonight Show* (because I was) and so I'd have to explain how much I like watching tapes of old programs at the Museum of Television and Radio and I don't want to get too personal.

It seems that all three of them attended a Boston Pops concert at Tanglewood the previous evening, and they chat about the conductor. This, I think, is my in. I, too, enjoy being entertained.

Relieved to have something, anything, to say, I pipe up, "I went to the Berkshire Theatre Festival last night."

"Oh, did you see *Peter Pan?*" the woman asks.

"No," I say. *"Assassins!"*

"What's that?" wonders the Englishman.

To make up for the fact that I've been clammed up and moping I speak too fast, merrily chirping, "It's the Stephen Sondheim musical in which a bunch of presidential assassins and would-be assassins sing songs about how much better their lives would be if they could gun down a president."

"Oh," remarks Mr. Connecticut. "How was it?"

"Oh my god," I gush. "Even though the actors were mostly college kids, I thought it was great! The orange-haired guy who played the man who wanted to fly a plane into Nixon was hilarious. And I found myself strangely smitten with John Wilkes Booth; every time he looked in my direction I could feel myself blush." Apparently, talking about going to the Museum of Television and Radio is "too personal," but I seem to have no problem revealing my crush on the man who murdered Lincoln.

Now, a person with sharper social skills than I might have noticed that as these folks ate their freshly baked blueberry muffins and admired the bed-and-breakfast's teapot collec-

3

tion, they probably didn't want to think about presidential gunshot wounds. But when I'm around strangers, I turn into a conversational Mount St. Helens. I'm dormant, dormant, quiet, quiet, old-guy loners build log cabins on the slopes of my silence and then, boom, it's 1980. Once I erupt, they'll be wiping my verbal ashes off their windshields as far away as North Dakota.

I continue. "But the main thing that surprised me was how romantic *Assassins* was."

"Romantic?" sneers a skeptic.

"Totally," I rebut. "There's a very tender love scene between Emma Goldman and Leon Czolgosz."

Blank stares.

"You know. He was the anarchist who killed McKinley. Buffalo? 1901? Anyway, the authorities initially suspected Goldman had helped him, but all it was was that he had heard her speak a couple of times about sticking it to The Man. He'd met her, but she wasn't his co-conspirator. Anyway, the play dramatizes the moment they meet. He stops her on the street to tell her that he loves her. The guy who played Czolgosz was wonderful. He had this smoldering Eastern European accent. Actually, he sounded a lot like Dracula— but in a good way, if you know what I mean." (They don't.)

"He told her, 'Miss Goldman, I am in love with you.' She answered that she didn't have time to be in love with him. Which was cute. But, this was my one misgiving about the performance, I thought that the woman playing Goldman was too ladylike, too much of a wallflower. Wasn't Emma Goldman loud and brash and all gung ho? Here was a woman whose words inspired a guy to kill a president. And come to think of it, one of her old boyfriends shot the industrialist

Henry Frick. Maybe I'm too swayed by the way Maureen Stapleton played Goldman in the film *Reds*. She was so bossy! And remember Stapleton in that Woody Allen movie, *Interiors*? Geraldine Page is all beige this and bland that so her husband divorces her and hooks up with noisy, klutzy Maureen Stapleton, who laughs too loud and smashes pottery and wears a blood-red dress to symbolize that she is Alive, capital A. Wait. I lost my train of thought. Where was I?"

Englishman: "I believe Dracula was in love with Maureen Stapleton."

"Oh, right. I haven't even mentioned the most touching part. Squeaky Fromme and John Hinckley sing this duet, a love song to Charles Manson and Jodie Foster. Hinckley and Squeaky sang that they would do anything for Charlie Manson and Jodie Foster. And I really believed them! Squeaky's like, 'I would crawl belly-deep through hell,' and Hinckley's all, 'Baby, I'd die for you.' It was adorable."

Mr. Connecticut looks at his watch and I simultaneously realize that I've said way too much and that saying way too much means I might miss my bus back home. And I really want to go home. I yell, "Nice meeting you!" and nearly knock down the teapot collection in my rush to get away from them. Though before I can leave, I have to settle up my bill with the friendly B&B owner. His first name? Hinckley.

On the bus home, I flip through my *Assassins* program from the night before and read the director's note. Of course talking about the murders of previous presidents is going to open the door to discussing the current president. That's what I like to call him, "the current president." I find it difficult to say or type his name, George W. Bush. I like to call him "the current president" because it's a hopeful phrase, implying that his administration is only temporary. Timothy Douglas, the *Assassins* director, doesn't say the president's name either, but he doesn't have to. Clearly, Douglas is horrified and exasperated by the Iraqi war. He writes,

> Proportionate to my own mounting frustrations at feeling increasingly excluded from the best interests of the current administration's control in these extraordinary times helps me toward a visceral understanding of the motivation of one who would perpetrate a violent act upon the leader of the free world. My capacity for this depth of empathy also gives me pause, for I have no idea how far away I am from the "invisible line" that separates me from a similar or identical purpose. . . . Please allow me to state for the record that I am completely against violence of any kind as a way of resolving conflicts.

That crafty explanation slaps me in the forehead with all the force of "duh." Until that moment, I hadn't realized that I embarked on the project of touring historic sites and monuments having to do with the assassinations of Lincoln, Garfield, and McKinley right around the time my country iffily went to war, which is to say right around the time my resentment of the current president cranked up into contempt. Not that I want the current president killed. Like that director, I will, for the record (and for the FBI agent assigned to read this and make sure I mean no harm—hello there), clearly state that while I am obsessed with death, I am against it.

Like director Tim Douglas, my simmering rage against

the current president scares me. I am a more or less peaceful happy person whose lone act of violence as an adult was shoving a guy who spilled beer on me at a Sleater-Kinney concert. So if I can summon this much bitterness toward a presidential human being, I can sort of, kind of see how this amount of bile or more, teaming up with disappointment, unemployment, delusions of grandeur and mental illness, could prompt a crazier narcissistic creep to buy one of this country's widely available handguns. Not that I, I repeat, condone that. Like Lincoln, I would like to believe the ballot is stronger than the bullet. Then again, he said that before he got shot.

I am only slightly less astonished by the egotism of the assassins, the inflated self-esteem it requires to kill a president, than I am astonished by the men who run for president. These are people who have the gall to believe they can fix us—us and our deficit, our fossil fuels, our racism, poverty, our potholes and public schools. The egomania required to be president or a presidential assassin makes the two types brothers of sorts. Presidents and presidential assassins are like Las Vegas and Salt Lake City that way. Even though one city is all about sin and the other is all about salvation, they are identical, one-dimensional company towns built up out of the desert by the sheer will of true believers. The assassins and the presidents invite the same basic question: Just who do you think you are?

One of the books I read for McKinley research was Barbara Tuchman's great history of European and American events leading up to World War I, *The Proud Tower*. Her anarchism chapter enumerates the six heads of state who were assassinated in the two decades before Archduke Ferdinand was murdered in 1914: McKinley, the president of France, the empress of Austria, the king of Italy, a couple of Spanish premiers. Her point being, it was an age of assassination. Well, I can come up with at least that many assassinations off the top of my head from the last two years alone as if playing some particularly geopolitical game of Clue: Serbian prime minister (sniper in front of government building in Belgrade), Swedish foreign minister (stabbed while shopping in Stockholm), the Taiwanese president and vice president (wounded when shots were fired at their motorcade the day before an election), two Hamas leaders (Israeli missile strikes), president of the Iraqi Governing Council (suicide bomber). And, in May 2004, an audio recording surfaced from Osama bin Laden promising to pay ten thousand grams of gold (roughly $125K) to assassins of officials in Iraq representing the United States or the United Nations.

"I'm worried about the president's safety," I said at a Fourth of July party in 2004 when this guy Sam and I were talking about the upcoming Republican National Convention here in New York. "I think you've seen *The Manchurian Candidate* too many times," said Sam. Guilty. Still, I dread bodily harm coming to the current president because of my aforementioned aversion to murder, but also because I don't think I can stomach watching that man get turned into a martyr if he were killed. That's what happens. It's one of the few perks of assassination. In death, you get upgraded into a saint no matter how much people hated you in life. As the rueful Henry Adams, a civil service reform advocate who marveled at his fellow reformers' immediate deification of President Garfield after that assassination, wrote, "The cyn-

ical impudence with which the reformers have tried to man-
ufacture an ideal statesman out of the late shady politician
beats anything in novel-writing."

*

Somewhere on the road between museum displays of Lincoln's skull fragments and the ceramic tiles on which Garfield was gunned down and McKinley's bloodstained pj's
it occurred to me that there is a name for travel embarked
upon with the agenda of venerating relics: pilgrimage. The
medieval pilgrimage routes, in which Christians walked from
church to church to commune with the innards of saints, are
the beginnings of the modern tourism industry. Which is to
say that you can draw a more or less straight line from a Dark
Ages peasant blistering his feet trudging to a church display-
ing the Virgin Mary's dried-up breast milk to me vomiting
into a barf bag on a sightseeing boat headed toward the
prison-island hell where some Lincoln assassination conspirators were locked up in 1865.

I remembered that my friend Jack Hitt had written a book
called *Off the Road* in which he retraced the old pilgrimage
route to Santiago de Compostela in Spain. So I floated my
pilgrimage theory to him in an e-mail and he wrote back that
at one point on his Spanish trip, he saw "the flayed 'skin' of
Jesus—the entire thing, you know, with like eyeholes and
stuff, mounted on a wooden frame." Cool. His e-mail went
on to say that in the Middle Ages,

Relics were treasured as something close to the divine.
Often when a great monk died and there was a sense that
he might be canonized, the corpse was carefully guarded

9

in a tomb—often twenty-four hours a day. Visitors could come to the tomb. Most of the funeral vaults of potential saints had a small door, like you might have in your suburban house for cats. Visitors could poke their heads in the little door and breathe in the holy dust. Most people thought that such dust had curative powers since it was associated with a near-saint whose corporeal matter had been directly blessed by God. So, getting near a relic, touching it, being near it was considered extremely beneficial and treasured.

Curative powers? I wondered how taking the train to Philadelphia to look at a sliver of the Garfield assassin's brain floating in a jar is supposed to fix me. "There was a late Renaissance king of Spain whom I loved," Jack went on.

He was so inbred and crazy, incapable of eating food or reproducing that he was called *El Hechizado*—the bewitched. He was probably retarded. After destroying the world's largest empire (ever, in all history) and bankrupting a nation drowning in New World gold, he came to die. Half the College of Cardinals arrived to recite prayers over his feeble frail body. They split a live dove over his head every morning. And they had brought with them the most powerful curative tool then known to man, the putrefying, stinking rotting corpse of Saint Francis of Assisi, then (and maybe now) the greatest saint ever. It was laid in the bed next to *El Hechizado* and for the rest of his days, the King of Spain shared his bed with the greatest relic ever in the hopes that it would restore his health and grant him the potency to generate an heir. Neither happened and the empire eventually dissolved into warfare with England around 1588 and became a backwater.

I can relate. (Not to being retarded, though it has been my experience that if you go on your historical pilgrimage while wearing your *Jackass: The Movie* ball cap some people look at you like you are.) I crave my relics for the same reason Señor Bewitched bunked with the late saint. We're religious. I used to share the king's faith. And while I gave up God a long time ago, I never shook the habit of wanting to believe in something bigger and better than myself. So I replaced my creed of everlasting life with life, liberty, and the pursuit of happiness. "I believe in America," chants the first verse of one of my sacred texts, *The Godfather.* Not that I'm blind to the Psych 101 implications of trading in the martyred Jesus Christ (crucified on Good Friday) for the martyred Abraham Lincoln (shot on Good Friday).

One thing the Spanish king's Catholicism and my rickety patriotism have in common, besides the high body count, is that both faiths can get a little ethereal and abstract. Jesus and Lincoln, Moses and Jefferson can seem so long gone, so unbelievable, so dead. It's reassuring to be able to go look at something real, something you can put your hands on (though you might want to wash them afterward). "What's that smell?" wondered the bewitched king. Actual Saint Francis, staining the sheets. Did a fellow as shrewd and sad and poetic and miraculously the right man for the right job at the exact right moment as Abraham Lincoln truly walk the earth until gunned down? Well, come along on one of these We Cannot Escape History weekend escape packages and we'll genuflect before the bone from inside his head

and the hats he wore on top of his head. The Declaration of
Independence, the Constitution, the Civil War—when I really think about them they all seem about as likely as the
parting of the Red Sea. But somehow, jumping up a foot to
stare at my own face framed in Lincoln's Springfield shaving mirror makes the whole far-fetched, grisly, inspiring
story of the country seem more shocking and more true.
Especially since when I jumped up to the mirror, I set off a
super-loud alarm.

Jack's e-mail about the relics ended with an aside about
how he had just been shopping on eBay and stumbled onto
"a guy selling tiny specks of 'George Washington's hair.' Literally, these clippings were nothing more than single strands
of hair less than a quarter of an inch long. They came in
little ampoules and with documentation."

I looked away from my computer and over at a frame
on my wall and wrote Jack back that my twin sister Amy
had given me a teensy eyelash-size hair of John Brown as
a Christmas present. She settled on the more affordable
tresses of the abolitionist guerrilla warrior Brown because
Lincoln's hair was out of her price range. That is the kind of
person I have become, the kind of person who rips open a
package in snowman wrapping paper to discover that her
only sibling has bought her an executed slavery hater's hair.
(I got her a DVD player.)

As I learned that morning at the bed-and-breakfast while
I was going on and on about the singing Squeaky Fromme,
most people don't like to talk about violent historical death
over muffins. I would come to find out that's also true about
lunch and dinner too. When my friend Bennett and I were

trying to decide where to have brunch he suggested a dim sum place in Chinatown. He asked me if I had ever tried bubble tea. I said yes, that I think a better name for the tea afloat with tapioca globules is tea 'n' dumplings and that I had it at the Chinese restaurant in D.C. that used to be the boardinghouse where Booth and his co-conspirators met to plan the Lincoln assassination.

Bennett asked, "You know that Kevin Bacon game?"

"The one where he can be connected to every other movie star?"

"Yeah, that's the one. Assassinations are your Kevin Bacon. No matter what we're talking about, you will always bring the conversation back to a president getting shot."

He was right. An artist pal, marveling at the youth of a painter in the Whitney Biennial was subjected to the trivia, "Well, John Wilkes Booth was only twenty-six when he killed Lincoln." A gardener friend, bragging about his lilacs, was forced to endure a recitation of Walt Whitman's Lincoln death poem "When Lilacs Last in the Dooryard Bloom'd."

As Johnny Cash put it about how his Garfield assassination ballad went over at Carnegie Hall in 1962, "I did 'Mr. Garfield,' which isn't very funny if you're not on the right wavelength, and nobody was." Once I knew my dead presidents and I had become insufferable, I started to censor myself. There were a lot of get-togethers with friends where I didn't hear half of what was being said because I was sitting there, silently chiding myself, Don't bring up McKinley. Don't bring up McKinley.

The bright side to researching the first three presidential assassinations is that my interest is optional, a choice. One man who makes cameo appearances in all three stories was not so lucky. Abraham Lincoln's oldest son, Robert Todd Lincoln, was in close proximity to all three murders like some kind of jinxed Zelig of doom. The young man who wept at his father's deathbed in 1865 was only a few feet away when James A. Garfield was shot in a train station in 1881. In 1901, Robert arrived in Buffalo mere moments after William McKinley fell. Robert Todd Lincoln's status as a presidential death magnet weighed on him. Late in life, when he was asked to attend some White House function, he grumbled, "If only they knew, they wouldn't want me there."

On July 2, 2003, the 122nd anniversary of the Garfield assassination, my friend Nicole and I rented a car and drove up to Vermont to visit Hildene, Robert Todd Lincoln's estate in Manchester. His mansion is a museum with landscaped grounds where, in the winter, there is cross-country skiing. I find it hard to stop myself from being unfair to Robert. Shown around the house, climbing the graceful staircase a guide proudly points out Robert himself designed, it's impossible not to compare him with his father: Abraham Lincoln freed the slaves, Robert Lincoln bought a nice ski lodge.

The person I'm really treating unfairly is Nicole, for talking her into the eight-hour round-trip drive to Hildene. I guess learning trivia about when the colossal William Howard Taft came to visit he slept on the floor because he was afraid of breaking the bed in Robert Lincoln's guest room isn't enough for Nicole, because at the end of the day, she pronounces the trip "kind of a bust." Ever polite, she hastens to add, "You brought really good snacks, though."

When we return the rental car on Thirty-fourth Street,

the block is crawling with people filing into a concert at the Hammerstein Ballroom. The Foo Fighters are on the marquee. I walk Nicole to the subway, hoping she doesn't notice who's playing, because then she might remember tagging along as my plus-one to a Foo Fighters show seven years earlier, when I was still making a living as a rock critic, which I fear might remind her what I was like before I went off the historical tourism deep end, when tagging along with me to work used to be fun.

President Warren G. Harding, beware: the elderly Robert Lincoln was the guest of honor at the dedication ceremony at the Lincoln Memorial in 1922. (Harding, also in attendance, returned to the White House unscathed.) Robert died in 1926, but for the rest of his life, he made it a point to visit the memorial often, gazing into his father's marble eyes, saying, "Isn't it beautiful?"

A pilgrimage needs a destination. For medieval Christians, that was usually the cathedral of Saint James in northern Spain. This tour of the assassinations of Lincoln, Garfield, and McKinley ends up at the Lincoln Memorial because that's where I'm always ending up. It is the closest thing I have to a church.

On the National Mall in Washington, next to the Reflecting Pool, that shallow, rectangular pond in front of the Lincoln Memorial, the National Park Service has posted a sign. It features a picture of the protesters in the March on Washington listening to Martin Luther King Jr. deliver his "I have a dream" speech from the memorial's steps. The sign says, "The Pool reflects more than the sky and landscape. It mirrors the moods of America, from national celebrations to dramatic demonstrations." This reminds me of a photograph of the memorial's Lincoln sculpture that my tour guide held up at Chesterwood, Daniel Chester French's studio in the Berkshires.

French obsessed for years about how to sculpt Lincoln's peculiar face, fretting and reading and thinking before committing to the brooding, seated philosopher in the memorial. He received the commission in 1913. So by the time the memorial was finally dedicated nine years later, the sculptor was a little pent up worrying how his work would come off. Hoping to celebrate, French looked upon the final installation with horror. The problem with putting in a reflecting pool? The darn thing reflects. When the light off the Reflecting Pool bounced up onto Lincoln's face, it looked as if a flashlight had been held up under his chin. The Chesterwood guide described the photo as a "Halloween picture." Lincoln looks frightened, startled, confused—Edvard Munch's *The Scream* by way of Macaulay Culkin's *Home Alone*. Apparently, "hilarious" wasn't the aesthetic French had been going for.

Along with architect Henry Bacon, French tinkered with various solutions, concluding that only electric lighting placed above Lincoln's head could correct the travesty. For years, he pestered the government to pay to fix it. I'm happy for French that he lived long enough to see the ceiling lights installed so that his Lincoln is as dignified and pensive as he intended; otherwise the man might have died of embarrassment.

But I like that picture of the panicky Abraham Lincoln. Lately, I think I might prefer it. Given what that sign says about the Reflecting Pool mirroring American moods, and given that the current mood is on the edgy side what with all the new coffins being buried every day in the Arlington National Cemetery behind the statue's back, a freaked-out Lincoln gaping at the current government might look a little more true.

Then again, in the 1860s, at least half the country loathed Abraham Lincoln for filling up too many soldiers' coffins. Which is why Daniel Chester French isn't the only reason that marble likeness sits there on the Mall. John Wilkes Booth deserves some of the credit—a notion that would make the assassin want to throw up. After all, if no one had hated Lincoln, there would be no Lincoln Memorial to love.

The bullet that killed Lincoln (based on an undated allegorical lithograph in the collection of the Library of Congress, in which John Wilkes Booth is entombed inside his own ammo). The actual bullet that killed Lincoln is considerably more smushed and on display in the National Museum of Health and Medicine in Washington, D.C., next to bone fragments from the president's skull.

CHAPTER ONE

Going to Ford's Theatre to watch the play is like going to Hooters for the food. So I had intended to spend the first act of 1776, a musical about the Declaration of Independence, ignoring the stage and staring at Abraham Lincoln's box from my balcony seat. Then I was going to leave at intermission. Who wants to hear the founding fathers break into song? Me, it turns out. Between eloquent debates about the rights of man, these wiseacres in wigs traded surprisingly entertaining trash talk in which a deified future president like Thomas Jefferson is deplored as a "red-headed tombstone." George Washington's amusingly miserable letters from the front—New Jersey is full of whores giving his soldiers "the French disease"—are read aloud among the signers with eye-rolling contempt, followed by comments such as "That man would depress a hyena." Plus, Benjamin Franklin was played by the actor who played the Big Lebowski in *The Big Lebowski*. I was so sucked into 1776 that whole production numbers like "But, Mr. Adams" could go by and I wouldn't glance Lincolnward once, wrapped up in noticing that that second president could really sing.

Deciding to stay for act II, I spend intermission in the Lincoln Museum administered by the National Park Service in the theater's basement. There are the forlorn blood spots on the pillow thought to have cradled the dying Lincoln's head; the Lincoln mannequin wearing the clothes he was shot in; the key to the cell of conspirator Mary Surratt; the gloves worn by Major Henry Rathbone, who accompanied the Lincolns to the theater and was stabbed by Booth in the president's box; Booth's small, pretty derringer; and, because it's some kind of law for Lincoln-related sites to have them, sculptor Leonard Volk's cast of Lincoln's hands.

Intermission over, I found myself looking forward to the rest of the play, happily bounding back up to my seat. But I paused on the balcony stairs for a second, thinking about how these were the very stairs that Booth climbed to shoot at Lincoln and how sick is this? Then I remembered, oh no they're not. The interior of the Ford's Theatre in which Lincoln was shot collapsed in 1893, but then, in 1968, the National Park Service dedicated this restoration, duplicating the setting of one of the most repugnant moments in American history just so morbid looky-loos like me could sign up for April 14, 1865, as if it were some kind of assassination fantasy camp. So how sick is that?

Act II of 1776 isn't as funny as act I, and not just because Ben Franklin gets to crack fewer sex jokes. It's time for the slavery question. Jefferson and Adams want a document about liberty and equality to include a tangent denouncing kidnapping human beings and cramming them into floating jails only to be auctioned off and treated as animals. This is followed by the expected yelling of southerners who refuse to sign such hogwash, pointing out that slavery is in the Bible, their way of life, blah, blah. What's unexpected is the song. Edward Rutledge of South Carolina (his brother would go on to sign the Constitution) sings a strange but effective *j'accuse* called "Molasses to Rum," in which he implicates New England ships and merchants in the slave trade triangle, asking John Adams: Boston or Charleston, "Who stinketh most?"

This script as performed by these actors really does give the audience a feel for the anguish, embarrassment, and disappointment Adams and Jefferson went through yielding to the southerners' edit. "Posterity will never forgive us," Adams sighs, caving in.

Even though the scene couldn't be more gripping, my head snaps up away from the action to stare at Lincoln's box. The thing that makes seeing this play in Ford's Theatre more meaningful than anywhere else is that I can look from the stage to Lincoln's box and back again, and I can see exactly where this compromise in 1776 is pointing: into the back of Lincoln's head in 1865.

"This country was formed for the white, not for the black man," John Wilkes Booth reportedly wrote on the day he pulled the trigger. (I say reportedly because the letter, to the editors of a Washington newspaper, was destroyed in 1865 but later "reconstructed" and reprinted in 1881.) Booth (again, reportedly, but it sounds like him) continued, "And, looking upon African slavery from the same standpoint as the noble framers of our constitution, I, for one, have ever considered it one of the greatest blessings, both for themselves and us, that God ever bestowed upon a favored nation." So this is whom we're dealing with—not the raving madman of assassination lore, but a calculating, philosophical racist. Then again, anyone who has convinced himself that slavery is a "blessing" for the slaves is a little cracked.

After the play I take a walk to the Lincoln Memorial. It's late. Downtown D.C. is vacant this time of night. Like that of the Lincoln administration, this is a time of war. Back then, Union soldiers camped out on the Mall. Nowadays, ever since the attack on the Pentagon in 2001, the capital has been clamped down. How is this manifested? Giant planters blocking government buildings, giant planters barricading every other street. Theoretically, the concrete flowerpots are solid enough to fend off a truck bomb. And yet the effect is ridiculous, as if we believe we can protect ourselves from suicide bombers by hiding behind blooming pots of marigolds, flowers whose main defensive property is repelling rabbits.

I walk down the darkened Mall past the white protruding phallus that is the Washington Monument. It looks goofy enough in the light of day but ugliest at night, when the red lights at its tippy top blink so as to keep airplanes from crashing into it, a good idea I know, but still, those beady blinking eyes make it come across as fake and sad, the way robots used to look in old movies before George Lucas came along.

I'm alone out here. Even though the Mall is a pretty safe place, I've read way too many pulpy coroner novels with first sentences such as "I spent a long afternoon at the morgue," so I'm feeling a little mugable. Nervously, I shove my hands in my pockets. In the forensics novels the contents of a victim's pockets on the night of her death Say Something about her character. My Ford's Theatre ticket stub and Jimmy Carter key chain say that I am the corniest, goody-goody person in town. Luckily, I survived the evening unscathed so no one will ever find out about that losery Jimmy Carter key chain.

The Library of Congress has a whole display case of items in Lincoln's pockets when he died. His pocketknife, two pairs of spectacles, and a Confederate five-dollar bill are spread out on red velvet. They would probably display the lint too if someone had had the foresight to keep it. The items take on a strange significance. Those are the glasses he must have worn to read his beloved Shakespeare. He could have used the pocketknife to carve the apple he liked to eat for lunch.

The contents of John Wilkes Booth's pockets also get the glass case treatment. At Ford's Theatre, I looked at the five photographs of women in the womanizing Booth's pockets when he died, and I couldn't help but believe that I picked up new insight into his character, that he wasn't just a presidential killer, he was a lady-killer too. Four of the women were actresses he knew. The fifth picture captures Booth's secret fiancée, Lucy Hale, in profile. Lucy was spotted with Booth the morning of the assassination, probably around the same time her ex-senator father John P. Hale, Lincoln's newly appointed ambassador to Spain, was meeting with the president in the White House. Hale, a New Hampshire Republican, was the first abolitionist ever elected to the U.S. Senate. One reason he was so keen on absconding to Europe on a diplomatic appointment was to put an ocean between his pretty daughter and Booth, whom the senator knew to be a pro-slavery southern sympathizer and, worse, an actor. In fact, Hale would have preferred to marry Lucy off to another young man he had noticed admiring her—the president's twenty-one-year-old son, Robert Todd Lincoln.

The Lincoln Memorial is at its loveliest when the sun goes down. It glows. It's quiet. There are fewer people and the people who are here at this late hour are reverent and subdued, but happy. The lights bounce off the marble and onto their faces so that they glow too, their cheeks burned orange as if they've had a sip of that good bourbon with the pretty label brewed near the Kentucky creek where Lincoln was born.

I read the two Lincoln speeches that are chiseled in the wall in chronological order, Gettysburg first. Shuffling past the Lincoln statue, I pause under the white marble feet, swaying back and forth a little so it looks like his knees move. A moment of whimsy actually opens me up for the Second Inaugural, a speech that is all the things they say —prophetic, biblical, merciful, tough. The most famous phrase is the most presidential: with malice toward none. I revere those words. Reading them is a heartbreaker considering that a few weeks after Lincoln said them at the Capitol he was killed. But in my two favorite parts of the speech, Lincoln is sarcastic. He's a writer. And in his sarcasm and his writing, he is who he was. He starts off the speech reminding his audience of the circumstances of his First Inaugural at the eve of war. It's a (for him) long list, remarkably even-handed and restrained, pointing out that both the North and the South were praying to the same god, as if they were just a couple of football teams squaring off in the Super Bowl. Then things turn mischievous: "It may seem strange that any men should dare to ask a just God's assistance in wringing their bread from the sweat of other men's faces; but let us judge not that we be not judged." Know what that is? A zinger—a subtle, high-minded, morally superior zinger. I glance back at the Lincoln statue to see if his eyes have rolled. Then, at the end of this sneaky list of the way things were, he simply says, "And the war came." Kills me every time. Four little words to signify four long years. To call this an understatement is an understatement. To read this speech is to see how Lincoln's mind worked, to see how he governed, how he lived. There's the narrative buildup, the explanation, the lists of pros and cons; he came late to abolitionism, sought compromise, hoped to save the Union without war, etc., until all of a sudden the jig is up. The man who came up with that teensy but vast sentence, *And the war came,* a four-word sentence that summarizes how a couple of centuries of tiptoeing around evil finally stomped into war, a war he says is going to go on "until every drop of blood drawn with the lash, shall be paid by another drawn with the sword," is the same chief executive who in 1863 signed the Emancipation Proclamation. I've seen that paper. It's a couple of pages long. But after watching the slavery agony in 1776, I like to think of it as a postcard to Jefferson and Adams, another four-word sentence: *Wish you were here.*

When I used to get to the end of the Second Inaugural, in which Lincoln calls on himself and his countrymen "to do all which may achieve and cherish a just, and a lasting peace," I always wondered how anyone who heard those words could kill the person who wrote them. Because that day at the Capitol, Booth was there, attending the celebration as Lucy Hale's plus-one. In the famous Alexander Gardner photograph of Lincoln delivering the speech, you can spot Booth right above him, lurking. And what was Booth's reaction to hearing Lincoln's hopes for "binding up the nation's wounds"? Booth allegedly told a friend, "What an excellent chance I had to kill the president, if I had wished, on Inauguration Day!"

I used to march down the memorial's steps mourning the loss of the second term Lincoln would never serve. But I don't think that way anymore. Ever since I had to build those extra shelves in my apartment to accommodate all the books about presidential death—I like to call that corner of the hallway "the assassination nook"—I'm amazed Lincoln got to live as long as he did. In fact, I'm walking back to my room in the Willard Hotel, the same hotel where Lincoln had to sneak in through the ladies' entrance before his first inauguration because the Pinkerton detectives uncovered a plot to do him in in Baltimore before he even got off the train from Springfield. All through his presidency, according to his secretary John Hay, Lincoln kept a desk drawer full of death threats. Once, on horseback between the White House and his summer cottage on the outskirts of town, a bullet whizzed right by his head. So tonight, I leave the memorial knowing that the fact that Lincoln got to serve his whole first term is a kind of miracle.

*

Mary Surratt's D.C. boardinghouse, where John Wilkes Booth gathered his co-conspirators to plot Lincoln's death, is now a Chinese restaurant called Wok & Roll. I place an order for broccoli and bubble tea, then squint at an historic marker in front of the restaurant quoting Andrew Johnson that this was "the nest in which the egg was hatched." For her southern hospitality, Mrs. Surratt, who owned this boardinghouse as well as the tavern in Maryland where Booth would proceed after shooting Lincoln, would become the first woman executed by the U.S. government. She was hanged, along with George Atzerodt, David Herold, and Lewis Powell, in 1865. Here in her former boardinghouse sat Booth, Atzerodt, Herold, and Powell, along with Samuel Arnold, Michael

O'Laughlin, and Mary's weasel son John, who would hightail it to Europe after the assassination, leaving his mom to get strung up in his stead.

The plot to murder Abraham Lincoln started out as a plot to kidnap him, or rather it was one of several such kidnapping schemes. In their landmark study *Come Retribution*, William A. Tidwell, James O. Hall, and David Winfred Gaddy make a convincing case that John Wilkes Booth was a member of the Confederate Secret Service throughout the Civil War. Booth claimed to have been running messages and medicine across the lines for years, often traveling to and from Canada to confer with Confederate spooks up there. Booth was able to do this, to move freely between North and South, because he was a nationally famous actor, just as movie stars today get whisked through airport security while the rest of us stand in long lines taking off our shoes. The Confederates were shrewd to take advantage of Booth's fame. There is a lesson here for the terrorists of the world: if they really want to get ahead, they should put less energy into training illiterate ten-year-olds how to fire Kalashnikovs and start recruiting celebrities like George Clooney. I bet nobody's inspected that man's luggage since the second season of *ER*.

Tidwell, Hall, and Gaddy also persuasively and intriguingly argue that the plan to kidnap Lincoln had its origins as a retaliatory measure after it was discovered that Lincoln had authorized the capture of Jefferson Davis. Also, knowing how the Confederate ranks were thinning, General Grant had put a stop to prisoner of war exchanges. The South needed their dwindling stock of soldiers back more than the North. And so the notion of kidnapping President

Lincoln and exchanging him for southern POWs seemed logical and appealing, though by most accounts Davis himself seemed most aware of the consequences—that odds are, kidnapping the president of the United States is going to get said president killed. Even Davis thought himself above such dishonorable unpleasantness.

Then, on April 9, 1865, Appomattox. The war was winding down and the POWs would soon go home. Kidnapping Lincoln no longer served much purpose. There's no real consensus among historians as to when exactly the kidnapping plan turned into an assassination plot. It seems likely that Booth changed his mind first and then egged on his partners in crime. Booth and Powell were there on the White House lawn on April 11—a mere two days after Robert E. Lee surrendered to U. S. Grant—when Lincoln gave his speech on reconstruction. To me, this speech is unsatisfying, proposing to extend the right to vote to "very intelligent" blacks and/or those who fought for the Union—black *men* it goes without saying. But to Booth this halfhearted suggestion was the revelation of an electoral apocalypse. He told Powell, "That means nigger citizenship. Now, by god, I will put him through. That will be the last speech he will ever make." It was.

Booth's plan was to kill the nation's top three leaders so the federal government would dissolve into chaos. Booth would shoot Lincoln. George Atzerodt was to murder Vice President Johnson. (He chickened out at the last minute, so Johnson would live long enough to be impeached.) Lewis Powell was in charge of offing Secretary of State Seward. Booth's shooting of Lincoln tends to upstage these second-ary assassination plots, but the Seward episode is especially action-packed.

Around the same time Booth was at Ford's Theatre, Powell went to Seward's house on Lafayette Square. Seward was upstairs asleep in his sickbed, recovering from a well-publicized carriage accident a few days before in which he broke his jaw and an arm. Fanny Seward, his daughter, and soldier George Robinson were in the room watching over him.

Powell knocked on the door, talking his way in by claiming to be delivering medicine. He insisted on giving a pharmacist's package to Seward himself. Seward's son Frederick refused to let the stranger up the stairs. In her diary, Fanny, who had remained upstairs with her father, wrote, "Very soon, I heard the sounds of blows . . . sharp and heavy, with lighter ones in between." Powell had tried to shoot Frederick Seward, but his gun wouldn't fire. So Powell pistol-whipped him instead.

Powell ran up the stairs with the bleeding Fred on his heels. The two burst into Secretary Seward's room. Powell sliced at Seward with a Bowie knife. Fanny screamed. Robinson jumped Powell, pulling him off Seward. Powell decided to escape, hitting and slicing at the air willy-nilly. By the time he made it down the stairs and out the door, Powell had stabbed or pummeled Seward's other son Augustus and one of Seward's colleagues from the State Department. According to Fanny, "Blood, blood, my thoughts seemed drenched in it . . . it was on everything. The bed had been covered with blood—the blankets and sheet chopped with several blows of the knife."

Seward lived. He stayed on in Washington to serve as Andrew Johnson's secretary of state. After that he retired to his home in Auburn, in western New York. That house is now a museum in his honor.

The most riveting artifact at the William Seward House is part of the sheet from Seward's bed the night of the assassination. It's slashed and bloodstained. Considering that it is a memento of the worst night of their lives, I asked the museum director, Peter Wisbey, why the Sewards saved the bloodstained sheet.

The Sewards held on to everything, he says, adding, "I think saving the sheet was an act of family history preservation—especially since the assassination attempt had such dire consequences for so many of the family members." (Technically, everyone whom Powell attacked lived, though Seward's face would bear the scar from Powell's knife for the rest of his life, his son Fred would have a painful convalescence, and his wife, Frances, would die a few weeks after the attack, having never recovered from the shock.)

*

On February 12, my friend Bennett and I get up very early to make the six-thirty train to Washington to attend the Lincoln's Birthday wreath ceremony the National Park Service puts on at the Lincoln Memorial every year. The ceremony is very cold and very long—mostly elderly volunteers from archaic organizations placing donut-shaped flower arrangements at the Lincoln statue's feet. And because he had been such a good sport about getting up so early, I want to make it up to Bennett. After lunch at Old Ebbitt Grill, I settle up the bill and tell him, "I have a surprise for you."

I lead him around the corner to the Court of Claims Building. In the courtyard, past the fountain, I point at a plaque, chirping, "Ta-da! This was the site of Secretary of State Seward's house where he was stabbed in bed the night Lincoln was shot!"

Bennett looks at the plaque, then back at me, wondering, "This is my surprise? A plaque about Seward?"

"Uh-huh!"

He doesn't say anything for a while, just stands there reading the plaque, shaking his head. It says,

On this site Commodore John Rodgers built an elegant house in 1831. In it on April 14, 1865, an attempt was made to assassinate W. H. Seward, Secretary of State, by one of the conspirators who murdered Abraham Lincoln the same night.

Bennett looks at me, rolls his eyes, and silently trudges out of the courtyard.

I can theoretically grasp that a person might not get excited about a two-dimensional engraving attached to a government building marking the spot where the man who negotiated the purchase of Alaska was knifed by a friend of John Wilkes Booth. But this person? The person who was up for taking a six-thirty train in order to get to a Lincoln's 195th birthday wreath ceremony? The person who, come to think of it, also went with me to Gettysburg for the 137th anniversary of the reading of the Gettysburg Address? The person who was so excited when we went to the Reagan Presidential Library even though I found it a little disappointing in terms of scholarship? Who three hours earlier, as we were walking past the Library of Congress, pointed at some wormy stonework and taught me the word "vermiculation"? The person with whom I have spent Saturday night at the chess club chatting with a man who went to Reykjavik with Bobby Fischer for his match against Boris Spassky?

I pride myself on knowing my audience, so I'm shaken by Bennett's indifference. As he trudges out of the courtyard I harangue him with what I think are other juicy facts about buildings on Lafayette Square, such as, "Right next door: Mark Hanna's house!"

"Who was he?"

"Only William McKinley's best friend!" Surprisingly, this info also bombs.

Back home in New York, I'm not ready to give up on making a case for the Seward plaque. I love that thing. I e-mail Bennett the next morning that the Court of Claims Building, where the Seward plaque is hung, was designed by John Carl Warnecke, the architect who helped Jacqueline Kennedy with her historic preservation crusade to save Lafayette Square. After JFK was killed, Mrs. Kennedy hired Warnecke to design his grave at Arlington. In the process (I guess there's nothing more romantic than poring over graveyard designs), she and Warnecke fell in love. She was having an affair with the man in charge of her slain husband's tomb. For some reason, Bennett seems to think this sex and death gossip is more interesting than the Seward plaque.

"Seward plaque," by the way, has become our synonym for disappointment. When I break it to Bennett that I'm having trouble getting *Fiddler on the Roof* tickets, a musical he's keen on seeing because it reminds him of his grandmother's flight from the shtetl, he answers, "Whatever. I can take it. My people have been getting Seward plaqued for millennia."

Underneath the plaque about Powell's attack, there's another Seward plaque commemorating March 30, 1867, when Seward, by then Andrew Johnson's secretary of state, signed the treaty with Russia to purchase what is now the state of Alaska, though it would be disparaged as "Seward's Folly" and "Seward's Icebox" for years.

In 1869, Seward took a trip to Alaska to see what he had bought. One of the stops on his tour was Tongass Island, where the Tlingit tribe threw him one of their famous potlatches, a ceremony of gift giving.

A totem pole commemorates that night. Nowadays, the Seward pole stands in Saxman Village outside of Ketchikan. When I visited the village, my tour guide, Bill, explained that, unbeknownst to Seward, a potlatch is not a one-night party. Chief Ebbit of the Tlingits sent Seward on his way with "four or five skiploads of gifts—totem poles, canoes. Seward went off with a smile and a wave." After three years went by, Bill continues, Chief Ebbit was still waiting for Seward to come back and return the favor. Bill sums up the point of the potlatch as, "Let's say I give you a Volkswagen. Then you give me a Jaguar." Chief Ebbit never got his Jag. So after seven years of waiting in vain for a return on his investment, the chief commissioned a shame pole in Seward's honor. That is why the little Seward on top of the Seward totem pole has red paint on his face.

Seward's neighbor in the Saxman Native Village Totem Park is his old boss, Abraham Lincoln. The Abraham Lincoln totem pole here is a spruced-up replica of the weathered original in a museum up in Juneau. Here's one story about the pole: After the U.S. purchase of Alaska, an American military cutter came across two factions of warring Tlingits. The winners were about to enslave the losers.

Alaska natives, especially the warlike Tlingit tribes, were unapologetically brutal slave mongers of one another. An Englishman traveling among them while Alaska was still a Russian outpost once described a sort of slave potlatch in which two native slave owners, trying to prove their social status the way massive quantities of blankets would be given away in a potlatch, started shooting their slaves in a deadly spree of one-upmanship. When ten of the slaves were lying there dead, their owners just walked off and left them on the ground because it was considered crass behavior to touch the corpse of a slave. So the Englishman buried the dead slaves himself.

Slavery, it's worth remembering, wasn't a European import, but native to American shores. Most of the American Indians enslaved one another as war booty. Then the southeastern tribes, aping their southern white neighbors, owned black slaves, took their slaves west with them when the U.S. government removed them to Oklahoma. This is actually why I'm technically eligible for membership in the Daughters of the Confederacy—because my slave-owning Indian great-grandfather fought in Arkansas at the Battle of Pea Ridge with the Cherokee Mounted Volunteers in the Confederate Army. And while I am not proud of this Indian slavery footnote—it sickens me—I do not mind bringing it up because it illustrates that American Indians aren't just sappy cartoons of goodness as seen in the famous 1970s TV commercial in which garbage makes an Indian cry. I inherited my family's copy of *Laws of the Cherokee Nation,* published in 1875, and there is, for instance, a statute outlawing murder, presumably because even the oh-so-noble Cherokee were capable of homicide. Same thing with the Tlingit and their neighbors. They weren't just woodcarvers. They were fighters, fighters with flaws.

As for the cutter happening upon the Tlingit victors about to enslave the vanquished, supposedly the ship's captain broke up the fight. He announced to the newly enslaved that they were now living in the United States of America. And in the United States of America, a president named Abraham Lincoln had come along and freed the slaves. There is no more slavery in the United States, he said, and Alaska was a U.S. territory, so live free my Tlingit brothers. Thus the freed Tlingits went home and erected a totem pole in honor of this Lincoln, their emancipator.

That's a cute story. *Sunset* magazine published it in 1924. Turns out to be hooey. Alaska scholars believe there are two possible explanations for the Lincoln totem pole. The first is that it simply commemorates the tribe's first sighting of a white man and that the carver borrowed the only picture of a white man available—a photograph of Abraham Lincoln at Antietam. Another more interesting option is that the pole was erected after the American ship freed those slaves, but it was erected as a shame pole, a pole in honor of the thief who let the booty get away—the "Lincoln took my stuff" theory.

I'm not sure which story I believe, but I find all the explanations interesting—sad, ironic, bitter too. But there is nothing bitter, nothing ironic about standing in the Saxman park and looking at those magnificent totems. There on that Alaskan island dark green with trees, totems are still carved. I have the privilege of watching Nathan Jackson—a Tlingit carver so revered and skilled he is one of the few non-dead people to have appeared on a U.S. postage stamp—use a tool called an adze on a long new log.

There was a lovely moment when Bill the tour guide, supervising us poking around the grounds, noticed a raw tree trunk waiting to be carved, and spray-painted in turquoise on the rings was the name "Nathan." It was like watching a Renaissance Florentine come across a chunk of marble marked "Michelangelo."

The Seward pole is insult comedy—a little dwarf of a man perched on an upside-down bentwood box, symbolizing the way he stiffed the chief by failing to return the kindness of a potlatch. But the Lincoln pole—that I love, a long, tall shaft painted and carved at the base with the faces of a bear and ravens. In between the animals on the bottom and the Lincoln on top, the length of the pole is unpainted and bare so that you get a sense of the tree it used to be. Lincoln, charmingly short and squat, arms akimbo, is a happy, welcoming man. Even if that's not what he's supposed to look like, even if he's the harbinger of the white men showing up to outlaw the potlatch and take the land, that's how he looks—friendly. It's one of the rare Lincoln sculptures that capture the winking, joshing, fun-to-be-with side of his personality.

Staring up at the Lincoln pole I can't help but think of Edwin Markham's poem "Lincoln, Man of the People," which Markham read aloud at the dedication of the Lincoln Memorial. It ends with the poet's thoughts on what the death of such a man as Lincoln felt like:

As when a lordly cedar, green with boughs,
Goes down with a great shout upon the hills,
And leaves a lonesome place against the sky.

Interestingly, there's another replica of the Lincoln totem pole at the Illinois State Museum in Springfield. Cast in fiberglass, the "wood" of the pole is represented by very brown paint. Which is therefore the color of Lincoln's skin. In other words, in the copy of a totem pole that may be a shame pole attacking Lincoln for foiling the acquisition of new slaves, Lincoln looks like a black man.

*

There is one more peculiar American Indian–William H. Seward connection. It has to do with Seward's attacker, Lewis Thornton Powell, and the thousands of American Indian skeletal remains that used to be kept in storage at the Smithsonian and other museums.

The Native American Grave Protection and Repatriation Act of 1990 enabled Indian tribes to come east to identify the remains of their kinsmen whom anthropologists had pirated off to Washington, and take the remains back to tribal lands to be reburied. The repatriation of remains program was a long time coming, a bureaucratic solution to the sort of racist idiocy that allowed human remains to be essentially shoved into filing cabinets like dinosaur eggs or dried ferns. That Anglo scientists would cart off the dead to study them probably didn't surprise the tribes, considering that a lot of Indians were appalled and confused by the white men's ability to move away from the tombs of their ancestors. "Your dead cease to love you," Chief Seattle of the Duwamish said to the whites, pleading for the right to stay and live among his tribe's more affectionate ghosts.

In 1992, a researcher at the Smithsonian's National Museum of Natural History was cataloging bones so that tribes could claim them. He came across a skull identified with Powell's name. Coincidentally, the researcher had previously worked at Ford's Theatre.

Powell, the researcher knew, had been a Confederate soldier. Also known under the alias of Paine, Powell had served at Gettysburg and then with John Mosby's Rangers (known for raiding Union supply wagons and trains) before joining up with Booth, only to be hanged. The researcher then tracked down a woman whom he believed to be Powell's closest living relative, a great-niece in Florida. The niece requested the skull, hoping to bury it in the Seminole County cemetery where Powell's mother was laid to rest. Then, another woman came forward claiming to be an even closer relative than the niece. That woman, a Canadian, claimed to be Powell's great-granddaughter. She requested that her identity remain a secret, and as far as I can tell, the Smithsonian honored her request. She claimed that her great-grandmother was pregnant with Powell's illegitimate child when he was executed. The pregnant woman took off for Canada, where she bore his daughter.

I find the possibility of an impregnated girlfriend entirely plausible. Booth's good looks get a lot of play, but in a Lincoln conspirators' beauty pageant, my money's on Powell taking home the tiara. I remember the first time I saw him. It was in an art gallery at an exhibition of crime photos. Amidst the images of a strangler's hands and the source photo of the electric chair that Andy Warhol used in his paintings, there was a picture of Powell, a very tall, very handsome man. Who's *that*? I wondered. He smoldered, decked out in a jaunty, crumpled, double-breasted trench coat, staring at the camera dead-on. I was unaware of the man's identity, and thus what he had done to Seward, so the way he was reaching into his pocket struck me as gallant, as if he were Cary Grant pulling out a monogrammed cigarette case to offer a dame a smoke. Of course, right after that picture was taken, the government strung up Powell's pretty neck.

Powell's alleged great-granddaughter wanted the Smithsonian to keep the disputed skull. But eventually, the mystery woman backed off, and, after interinstitutional haggling about whether or not to keep the skull or "deaccession" it to the niece for burial, the niece ended up with the skull in 1994, burying it next to Powell's mother as she had promised.

I've seen Powell's grave. When my sister Amy and I were in Florida taking my nephew Owen to Disney World, we made a side trip to the Geneva Cemetery. The whole reason I wanted to take Owen to Disney World is that I fear that someday he's going to look through his childhood photo album and wonder why all his vacations with his aunt took place at places like the McKinley Memorial and Wounded Knee. And yet here we are. Powell's cemetery was just too close to Cinderella's Castle for me to pass up.

Amy drives past a feed store and a church whose sign out front reads, "Heaven is near. So's hell. Choose your destination daily." She continues past palm trees and Spanish moss, turning onto Cemetery Road. Earlier, I had written "Cemetery Road" in black ink on my hand to remind me that's the road the cemetery is on. When Owen grabbed my hand and asked what it said, I told him, but he didn't believe me, saying, "No, it doesn't say that." What does it say then? "It says that Halloween is coming soon!"

We extract Owen from his car seat and the three of us stand under some pine trees, looking at Powell's mother's grave, and Powell's. His is decorated with a cross marked "CSA" (Confederate States of America) and a Confederate flag. This is what it says:

PVT. LEWIS THORNTON POWELL, CSA
APRIL 22, 1844–JULY 7, 1865
2ND FLORIDA INFANTRY CO. 1
"HAMILTON BLUES"
43RD BATTALION VIRGINIA CALVARY [SIC]
"MOSBY'S RANGERS"

"They don't make any mention that he was a bad guy," Amy says.

"They usually don't—not on a tombstone anyway," I say.

Owen asks if there's a guy underground in a coffin.

"Just his skull," I answer. "Remember that word I taught you at Christmas? 'Decapitated'?" We were playing knights, fighting each other with plastic swords. Owen was winning. I was doubled over onto my parents' living room floor and he was pretending to slice my head off with his sword. Trying to be an educational aunt, or as educational as a person can be when a three-year-old is trying to chop her head off, I told him that the act of chopping off a person's head is called "decapitation" and that a head that's been chopped off is called "decapitated."

Owen, slicing at my neck like salami, insisted, "No it's not. It's called meat."

Standing there at Powell's grave, telling my nephew about a buried skull, I realize how much of our relationship revolves around body parts and severed heads. Once Owen learned to walk, we started playing a game I call Frankenstein, in which I am Frankenstein's monster and I chase him around trying to harvest his organs and appendages because my master is building another boy. "Frankenstein needs your spleen," I yell, aping the voice of an announcer at a monster truck rally. "Give me your spleen!" Which is why the seemingly gross book I gave him for his birthday, a collection of poetry for children called *The Blood-Hungry Spleen* was actually a sentimental choice, even though my sister tells me it didn't go over so well when he brought it to preschool.

Looking around Powell's cemetery, Owen sounds a little disappointed when he says, "It's not so scary here."

"Snake!" I yell. This isn't some shameless ploy to entertain him. As we stare at the grave of an attempted murderer, a black snake wraps itself around my left leg. "Is he a man-eater?" Owen wants to know. I'm sure as hell not going to find out, leaping special-effects-high into the air. Owen cannot stop laughing at my flailing. Just my luck, he prefers physical comedy. In fact, he adds the incident to his storytelling repertoire, repeatedly windmilling his arms, giggling, and jumping up and down, telling everyone he meets, "Aunt Sarah, she see snake and she say, 'Ah! Ah! Ah!' "

*

In Washington, D.C., directly across Lafayette Park from the house where Powell stabbed Seward, is a block of lovely brick row houses sheltering pet projects of the executive branch. The former home of Henry and Clara Rathbone is at 712 Madison Place. Today, it's the Office of the President's Council on White House Fellowships. (Secretary of State Colin Powell was a White House Fellow once. I remember I looked into applying for the program when I was younger, dropping the idea once I saw then-General Powell's name on the alumni list, realizing they were probably not looking for someone whose most impressive résumé line was "college radio DJ.")

Shuddering as I pass the building next door (Office for Obliterating the Separation of Church and State So That Our Tax Dollars Fund Churches Which Are Already Annoyingly Tax Exempt), I go inside, asking the receptionist to confirm if this was once the house of Major Henry Rathbone.

"I don't know," she answers. "Who's he?"

I tell her that Henry Rathbone and his fiancée/stepsister Clara Harris were in the box with the Lincolns the night of the assassination; that Rathbone was the first person to realize what Booth had done; that when he tried to stop Booth from escaping, Booth knifed Rathbone's arm.

"Around here," she says, "for someone like that, there's usually a plaque."

I tell her that Rathbone never fully recovered; that he was actually blamed for not stopping Booth; that he went slowly insane; that Clara married him anyway and had his children; that when Henry insisted on moving to Germany, she agreed, hoping the change would do him good; that crazy Henry shot and killed Clara in Germany just as Booth had shot Lincoln; that he would have killed their children too if a nanny hadn't stopped him; that by the way one of those kids lived to become the congressman from Illinois who, in

1926, introduced the bill to purchase the collection of artifacts in the Ford's Theatre Lincoln Museum; that Henry
was committed to a German insane asylum, which is where
he died; and that they don't really put up plaques about
things like that, though Thomas Mallon did write a good
novel on the subject called *Henry and Clara*.

"Oh, that guy," says the receptionist. "Yes, he lived here."

She says she's interested in reading the novel I mentioned, asks me to repeat its title. On the notepad she uses to
take while-you-were-out messages, she jots down *Henry and
Clara,* as if her boss is supposed to call them back.

*

Henry Rathbone and Clara Harris were not Mrs. Lincoln's
first choices for theater companions. Booth read in the
newspaper that Mr. and Mrs. Ulysses S. Grant would be ac-
companying the Lincolns to Ford's, but the general and his
wife backed out. Still, April 14 was a nice day for the Lincolns. Early that morning, their eldest son, Robert, showed
up. After graduating from Harvard, Robert had passed the
final few months of the war as a captain on General Grant's
personal staff. (That Robert sat out most of the war at Harvard was a political liability for his father, considering how
willing he was to send other people's sons to the front. But
Mrs. Lincoln had lost one of Robert's little brothers in
Springfield and another in the White House, so when she
begged the president to spare their firstborn, Lincoln gave
in. She tolerated Robert's position with Grant because it was
a cushy gig mostly involving escorting bigwigs who came to
visit.) Robert was with General Grant at Appomattox. And at
breakfast that morning he told his father about meeting

Robert E. Lee. In the afternoon, Mr. and Mrs. Lincoln took a carriage ride, both of them vowing to lighten up a little now that the war was over.

Lincoln was late for his own assassination. The play, Tom Taylor's *Our American Cousin,* had already started by the time the president and the first lady, along with Rathbone and Harris, arrived at the theater. Seeing the party enter the presidential box, the audience, along with the actors on stage, applauded the president.

Surely the plot appealed to Lincoln. The story of a comical American rube bumbling amidst his aristocratic English relatives must have reminded the occupant of the Executive Mansion of his rail-splitting, log cabin past. In fact, Booth, who knew the play well, timed his shot to coincide with a surefire laugh line. (It is a comfort of sorts to know that the bullet hit Lincoln mid-guffaw. Considering how the war had weighed on him, at least his last conscious moment was a hoot.)

At Ford's Theatre, I notice that the National Park ranger who delivers the tour does not quote the laugh line. After the tour, I go up and ask him why not.

"Tell you what," he says. "I'll tell you the line. You decide if it's funny." Then, pretending to be the character Lord Dundreary, calling after a Mrs. Mountchessington (who had just accused him of "not being used to the manners of good society"), "'Don't know the manners of good society, eh? Wal, I guess I know enough to turn you inside out, old gal— you sockdologizing old man-trap.'"

I don't laugh, it's true. I ask what "sockdologizing" means and he and his fellow ranger discuss having looked it up in various old dictionaries. "It means 'manipulative,'" he says.

I ask if the spirit of it is more "you lying son of a bitch" manipulative or "gosh darn you" manipulative. One ranger says the latter, the other says the former.

Whatever the nuance of "sockdologizing" was, after the line, then the laugh, the subsequent events happened fast. The ranger, when he was telling the story of Booth's jump to the stage, held an imaginary dagger, yelling *"Sic semper tyrannis!"*

Various people rushed to Lincoln, including the star of the play, actress Laura Keene, whose bloodstained collar is on display, along with the top hat Lincoln wore to the theater, in the Smithsonian's National Museum of American History.

When a doctor was called for, Charles Sabin Taft, an army surgeon attending the play, was lifted up to Lincoln's box. Taft asked that Lincoln be removed to the nearest home, which turned out to be the Petersen boardinghouse, across the street, now better known as The House Where Lincoln Died.

Lincoln was laid diagonally across a bed—the original is on display in the Chicago Historical Society. Surgeon General Barnes arrived, probing for the bullet. Robert Todd Lincoln was summoned from the White House, along with Lincoln's young secretary, John Hay. Secretary of War Edwin Stanton showed up too, famously pronouncing the next morning, after Lincoln's last breath, that "now he belongs to the ages."

Luckily, Dr. Taft went straight home and described his night in his diary, which is now in the special collections of McGill University in Montreal, thanks to an alumnus who bequeathed his collection of Lincolniana to his alma mater.

I happened to be in Montreal to do a reading at the annual Just for Laughs Comedy Festival, so I swung by the library to look at Taft's book. He wrote, "I remained with the President until he died, engaged during a greater part of the night in supporting his head so that the wound should not press upon the pillow and the flow of blood be obstructed." Oh, the agony of hours and hours of holding up the weight of Lincoln's head. The next day, surely Taft's arms were sore, so sore I'd imagine that every time he had to lift something, reach for the salt shaker, say, he would throb with the muscle memory of Lincoln's heavy head.

I find it strange that such an evocative artifact of the Lincoln assassination is archived in Canadian exile. But that night at the comedy festival, as I listened to American comic Rich Hall sing a country song he wrote about the current president called "Let's Get Together and Kill George Bush," a song the audience of Quebeckers loudly adored, I remembered that Canada in general and Montreal in particular were thick with Confederate Secret Service agents during the Civil War. John Wilkes Booth himself used to come here to conspire. So I took a stroll in the neighborhood in which Booth was known to lurk, the old part of Montreal known as "Old Montreal." Walking in Booth's footsteps, I was thinking of Lincoln's head.

*

From the Petersen boardinghouse, a hearse took Lincoln's body back to the White House. There, army surgeons Joseph Janvier Woodward and Edward Curtis performed the autopsy. Addressed to Surgeon General Barnes, Woodward's official report is by the book, so specifically scientific I had to consult a dictionary to understand it. Parts of Lincoln's face are "ecchymosed"—swollen. His brain is "pultaceous," which means, according to the *Shorter OED*, "semifluid, pulpy." It must have been a great relief for Woodward to hide behind words like that, the august Latinate words of his profession—"pultaceous" being as distant as ancient Rome compared to the horrifying here and now of "pulpy."

In Washington, far from the National Mall, artifacts from the Lincoln autopsy are on display in what used to be the Army Medical Museum. Now known as the National Museum of Health and Medicine, it's located on the campus of the Walter Reed Army Medical Center. To get in, one passes through a military checkpoint.

Being searched and questioned by camo-clad armed soldiers is disquieting enough if you are a small, meek white woman whose bag contains nothing more menacing than a Lemony Snicket novel and cinnamon gum; but if you are the Arabic-speaking cabdriver who drives her there and you are ordered to get out of the car to open the hood, the sweat starts to spurt off your forehead as if your turban is wound out of a garden hose that just got turned on. Maybe the terror of getting past the checkpoint is part of the medical museum experience: rattled and perspiring, once you finally get inside the cool, dark building, you feel so lucky to be alive that the display about Civil War scabies seems less depressing.

The exhibition devoted to Civil War medicine is called "To Bind Up the Nation's Wounds," a play on a line from Lincoln's Second Inaugural Address. Still, the display case devoted to his assassination is shoved to the side. It could be easily missed. Dr. Woodward, he of "pultaceous" and "ecchymosed," would approve of the clinical arrangement. Lincoln's skull fragments—the little pieces of bone that shattered when Booth's bullet made impact—are contained in what looks like a Petri dish. The probe Surgeon General Barnes used to locate the bullet lies there next to a teensy gray metal blob matter-of-factly labeled "The bullet that took the president's life."

My head tells me autopsies after murders are routine, that before Ford's Theatre turned into a shrine it was a crime scene, that of course the evidence of the crime was analyzed, then archived, that Abraham Lincoln was not just a martyr or a myth but a case file, what the pros nowadays call a "vic." So the evidence here calls up the corporeal presence of Lincoln (pieces of his head—*gross*) and Booth, who bought this very bullet, put said bullet in his pistol, then into Lincoln, which struck the skull, thereby chipping off these little pieces of it, mashing the bullet itself. These well-labeled, well-lit artifacts also suggest the existence of: the autopsy surgeon, the file clerk who catalogued and stowed them, the curator who decided to put them on display, the carpenter who built the display case, etc. Even though I am currently the only pilgrim paying my respects to the relics in this out-of-the-way museum, it suddenly feels pretty crowded in here, what with all the people who made this exhibit possible—from John Wilkes Booth on down to the intern who probably typed the labels—breathing down my neck. I can't make up my mind which step in the process is weirder, the murder or this display, unless the weirdest step of all is taking a fourteen-dollar cab ride to look at the display about the murder.

The "cuff stained with Lincoln's blood from the shirt of Edward Curtis who assisted in the autopsy" is there in the same case with the bullet and bones. After the procedure that stained his shirtsleeves, Curtis wrote a letter to his mother. It stands to reason that this doctor's letter to his mom is more vivid than his coworker's report to their boss. Curtis's description is everything Woodward's is not—physically, palpably aware of who the dead man was and what the dead man meant.

Curtis and Woodward were examining Lincoln's head, looking for the bullet, this bullet now in this museum. Curtis wrote, "Not finding it readily, we proceeded to remove the entire brain."

Think about that. I know I have. For the first few days after I read that, every time I took a five-dollar bill out of my wallet I looked at the engraving of Lincoln's head and couldn't get the image of his detached brain out of *my* head. Curtis goes on to write that as he was lifting the brain out of the skull, "suddenly the bullet dropped out through my fingers and fell, breaking the solemn silence of the room with its clatter, into an empty basin that was standing beneath." Listen. That room was so quiet. Of course it was. When the bullet dropped in such a quiet room, it must have been almost as jarring as the original gunshot. In less steady hands, the brain could have fumbled to the floor. Curtis stares at that bullet:

> There it lay upon the white china, a little black mass no bigger than the end of my finger—dull, motionless and harmless, yet the cause of such mighty changes in the world's history as we may perhaps never realize. . . . Silently, in one corner of the room, I prepared the brain for weighing. As I looked at the mass of soft gray and

white substance that I was carefully washing, it was impossible to realize that it was that mere clay upon whose workings, but the day before, rested the hopes of the nation. I felt more profoundly impressed than ever with the mystery of that unknown something which may be named "vital spark" as well as anything else, whose absence or presence makes all the immeasurable difference between an inert mass of matter owing obedience to no laws but those covering the physical and chemical forces of the universe, and on the other hand, a living brain by whose silent, subtle machinery a world may be ruled. The weighing of the brain . . . gave approximate results only, since there had been some loss of brain substance, in consequence of the wound, during the hours of life after the shooting. But the figures, as they were, seemed to show that the brain weight was not above the ordinary for a man of Lincoln's size.

*

On April 14, 1865, after President Lincoln RSVP'd for *Our American Cousin*, the theater manager draped an American flag in front of the presidential box. After Booth shot Lincoln and stabbed Henry Rathbone, Booth's spur caught on the flag as he jumped to the stage. The fall damaged Booth's leg but not his flair for drama. *"Sic semper tyrannis!"* he shouted. The state motto of Virginia, it means "Thus always to tyrants." Then, his horse waiting, Booth escaped, meeting up with co-conspirator David Herold. They were to ride through Maryland, toward the safety that was Virginia.

One Saturday morning, my friend Klam, who lives here in D.C., picks me up to drive Booth's escape route. One of

John Wilkes Booth's many faults is that he did not have the decency to die within walking distance of a Metro stop. I don't have a driver's license (phobia). So Klam is one of the many friends and family members I am always cajoling into chauffeuring me to glitzy assassination-related destinations. Plus, I purposefully invited along as many people I care about who would say yes because I thought it would keep me from objectifying my historical dead bodies. Like, if I were in the presence of loved ones whose deaths I dread, then I would be more likely to remember the grief of the loved ones of the dead presidents. I thought of it as the *Hamlet* approach. In the gravedigger scene in act V, Hamlet looks upon an anonymous skull and jokes that even Alexander the Great decomposed into dust that could have been used to plug a beer barrel. But when Hamlet is shown the skull of his old friend Yorick, the prince becomes unspeakably sentimental and sad because he knew him.

Klam is a writer who used to be a high school English teacher. I explain the above scenario, telling him that I'm Hamlet (without the suicidal tendencies) and he's Yorick's skull. I ask if he minds.

"I won't hold it against you unless you say I was driving and the rustling sound of my adult diapers was deafening." So, for the record, the rustling was rather faint, like riding shotgun next to a delicate hummingbird, a delicate hummingbird who, hearing his passenger's rhetorical question about why Booth had assassinated Lincoln to supposedly save the South instead of enlisting in the Confederate army, answers, "I totally get that impulse to do something big. It's why I quit short stories to write a novel."

Our first stop is the Surratt House Museum in Clinton,

Maryland. You wouldn't know it from looking, but this old wooden house isn't just a tourist trap for the historically curious. It's the Vatican of the Lincoln assassination subculture, hosting symposia, publishing scholarly books and journals.

Like a scene from a Western, Booth and Herold stopped here to pick up whiskey and guns. We came here to take a tour from a woman in period costume. Wearing a homemade hoop skirt, she's polite and welcoming, serene.

Having been around the block with regards to historical house tours, I have learned I learn more if I just clam up and listen. I've learned that the people who volunteer to preserve and interpret at such places are mostly local heroes who care deeply about their hometowns and the people who lived there before them. I have also learned that the people who spend a lot of time in these old houses care very much about the houses themselves—their architectural adornments, the household items that indicate past customs and ways of life. Though they're often dressed up in old-timey costumes, historical house guides often remind me of those modern painters who insisted a painting is first and foremost paint on canvas, not a picture of the world. A lot of house tours are about the thingness of things. For instance, when one visits Jefferson Davis's White House of the Confederacy in Richmond one learns that his bed was so short because most people back then slept sitting up; one doesn't hear much about how on earth Davis could sleep at all given the fact that he was waging a war to keep human beings enslaved. And when one visits Andrew Jackson's house in Nashville, one is more likely to hear about the painstaking restoration of the wallpaper and nothing much about how Jackson's policies sent one's Cherokee ancestors on the Trail of Tears.

And though our lovely hoopskirt wearer addresses the dastardly Booth in the tavern part of the house, she spends as much time walking us through the Surratt household's typical laundry day.

In the dining room, our guide shows us some heavy rocks of bread. Klam is for some reason very interested in the bread. She is delighted by his curiosity and rewards him with their name. "Maryland beaten biscuits," they're called. She tells him that she herself has baked the biscuits on occasion. And right when he starts pumping her for her recipe, I look at this pleasingly matronly woman in a hoopskirt tell my friend how to bake Maryland beaten biscuits, and I notice my friend is wearing an orange T-shirt emblazoned with the words PORN FREAK REHAB.

In the middle of a spiel about the sort of gentleman who dropped by the tavern to imbibe a glass or two with his fellows, our guide is called outside briefly to answer a coworker's question. Klam whispers, "You know what those guys would do? They'd sit around talking about whores. Then they'd spit and crap in the field. Then they'd rape a slave."

"Oh, I'm sure that's what she was about to say, Porn Freak."

I used to think John Waters movies were on the outlandish side until I came to Maryland. Klam and I stop for lunch at a dark roadside joint that feels like more of a throwback than the Surratt House ever could. The vegetable of the day is succotash to give you an idea. Technically, it's a family restaurant, but it will only remind you of your family if your mom chain-smoked menthols.

I can never make up my mind whether Maryland is off-beat or just off-putting. I probably would have felt that way if I were passing through in the 1860s too. While technically Maryland remained in the Union during the Civil War, it was *the* border state, a schizophrenic no-man's-land with the North at its door and the South in its heart.

Listen to its state song. Sung to the tune of the German Christmas carol "O Tannenbaum," "Maryland, My Maryland," was written as the Civil War was breaking out in 1861. The first line goes, "The despot's heel is on thy shore." Who is the despot? The new president, Lincoln, who, it's worth remembering, had to sneak into Washington for his inauguration so as to avoid the assassins waiting to jump him in Baltimore, a city which, in the song, is rhymed with "patriotic gore," commemorating the blood spilled on its streets on April 19, 1861, when a mob of local secessionists attacked a Massachusetts regiment passing through town. "Maryland, My Maryland," the song says, "spurns the Northern scum!" The song also calls for seceding from the Union, to stand by its sister state Virginia, going so far as to allude to that state's motto, *Sic semper tyrannis:*

> Virginia should not call in vain,
> Maryland!
> She meets her sisters on the plain—
> *Sic semper!* 'tis the proud refrain

Sic semper, of course, was the proud refrain hollered by Maryland's own John Wilkes Booth after making good on shooting the aforementioned "despot" Lincoln at war's end. One might think that a state song hinting at presidential assassination would have eerie echoes when that state's native son assassinated said president and therefore it might be headed for the title of "state song emeritus," the dustbin into which Virginia herself tossed its racist favorite "Carry Me Back to Old Virginny." But "Maryland, My Maryland" did not become the official state song until 1939. Despite the occasional nice try to ditch it, it remains the state song to this day.

All of which could just be written off as harmless symbolism, almost laughable anachronism. However, careful readers who are also symbolism devotees would have noticed that the date in 1861 when the Baltimore mob clashed with the Massachusetts soldiers was April 19—Patriot's Day—the anniversary of Lexington and Concord, when the first shots were fired in the Revolutionary War. It is also the anniversary of the Oklahoma City bombing in 1995.

When Timothy McVeigh bombed the Murrah Federal Building in Oklahoma City, he was wearing a T-shirt. On the back of the T-shirt, perhaps as a nod commemorating Patriot's Day, was the famous quote from Founding Father Thomas Jefferson, "The tree of liberty must be refreshed from time to time with the blood of patriots and tyrants." On the front of McVeigh's shirt was a picture of Abraham Lincoln. Printed under Lincoln's face was the caption "*Sic semper tyrannis.*" McVeigh ordered his shirt from a catalog sent out to subscribers of *Southern Partisan,* the pro-Confederate magazine. As if McVeigh wearing the shirt isn't disgusting enough, the catalog sold out of most sizes of the shirt *after* McVeigh made the news. People actually heard that a mass murderer responsible for 168 deaths was wearing clothing celebrating another murder and they wanted to dress up like him. According to media watchdogs Fairness and Accuracy in Reporting, by December of that year, the catalog reassured *Partisan* readers who had ordered the shirt:

> Due to a surprising demand for our anti-Lincoln T-shirt, our stock has been reduced to odd sizes. If the enclosed shirt will not suffice, we will be glad to refund your money or immediately ship you another equally militant shirt from our catalog.

And if the shirts were too big or too small, the readers could have cheered themselves up with one of the fetching, one-size-fits-all bumper stickers like "Clinton's military: a gay at every porthole, a fag in every foxhole."

If the shirt's popularity with readers of *Southern Partisan*, a magazine on the fringes, seems just that—on the fringes—three years after McVeigh inspired the shirt's commercial success, a Missouri senator would do an interview with the magazine announcing, "Your magazine also helps set the record straight. You've got a heritage of doing that, of defending Southern patriots like [Robert E.] Lee, [Stonewall] Jackson and [Confederate President Jefferson] Davis. Traditionalists must do more. I've got to do more. We've all got to stand up and speak in this respect, or else we'll be taught that these people were giving their lives, subscribing their sacred fortunes and their honor to some perverted agenda." And if that random senator still seems on the fringe, what with representing Missouri and/or kookily complaining about Jeff Davis's bad rap, it's worth noting that three years after saying that, the Missouri senator, John Ashcroft, became the attorney general of the United States, which is to say, the highest-ranking law enforcement official in all the land.

Meanwhile, in Charles County Maryland, Klam and I have finished lunch at Chez Succotash and are ready to resume the John Wilkes Booth escape route. About ninety minutes into the roughly ten-mile drive from the restaurant to the Dr. Samuel A. Mudd House, I become convinced of Mudd's guilt. Klam and I, armed with one road atlas, two historical maps of John Wilkes Booth's route, an old article from the *Washington Post* travel section, directions from various locals gassing up their cars, and six printouts from MapQuest.com, are lost for two hours. Mudd's house in rural Maryland is so hard to find, even in the daylight, even with a lap full of maps, that I don't see how Booth and Herold, who were horseback riding under the influence of the whiskey they acquired at the Surratt Tavern, could have found Mudd's house in the middle of the night if they didn't know exactly where they were going, and whom they could trust.

Booth arrived at Mudd's house in the middle of the night, seeking medical care for his broken leg. Days later, when Mudd was arrested for aiding and abetting the assassin, the doctor claimed that he didn't recognize the actor, that he was then unaware that Lincoln lay dying, and that in caring for a wounded man, even one who had just fatally wounded the president, Mudd was simply doing his Hippocratic duty. Though Mudd was convicted anyway, and shipped to the Fort Jefferson prison off the coast of Florida, he stuck to this story until the day he died. The mystery—did he or didn't he?—might have died with him but for the impressive tenacity of his grandson Richard Mudd.

Richard Mudd, who died in 2002 at the age of 101, was one of the greatest PR men of the twentieth century, doggedly lobbying to clear his grandfather's name. Two presidents who didn't agree on much concurred on Mudd. Though Jimmy Carter and Ronald Reagan concluded that the full presidential pardon Mudd received from Andrew Johnson in 1869 (for his heroic doctoring during a yellow fever outbreak at the prison) trumped all further presidential action, both Carter and Reagan wrote open letters to Richard Mudd expressing their faith in Dr. Mudd's innocence in the conspiracy. Carter wrote to Richard Mudd that he hoped to "restore dignity to your grandfather's name and clear the Mudd family name of any negative connotation or implied lack of honor," which Richard Mudd's distant cousin, journalist Roger Mudd, read on the evening news. Reagan wrote, "I came to believe as you do that Dr. Samuel Mudd was indeed innocent of any wrongdoing."

So there are two factions—those who believe Mudd was innocent and punished for simply doing his job, and those who believe Mudd was in bed with Booth from the get-go. I believe Mudd was guilty of conspiring with Booth in the original plot to kidnap Lincoln. And for history buffs leaning toward Mudd's guilt, or any fan of what I like to call the Emphasis Added School of History, Edward Steers's book *His Name Is Still Mudd: The Case Against Dr. Samuel Alexander Mudd* is both useful and appealing.

Steers recounts that Booth and Mudd were seen in public together on two occasions prior to the assassination, damning evidence the prosecution used to convict Mudd in 1865. Steers also brings up relatively new evidence, not unearthed from an archive until 1975, that Booth's co-conspirator George Atzerodt confessed that before the assassination, Booth had sent supplies ahead to Mudd's home. Moreover, the author persuasively argues that Mudd acted as Booth's "recruiter," introducing him to Confederate Secret Service agents, including John Surratt. Steers asserts that the historical record is silent on whether or not Mudd was in on the assassination, but he does point out that Mudd probably knew that his involvement in the original kidnapping plot was damning enough, and that if the doctor turned over the assassin to the authorities, the assassin would have implicated the doctor for sure. As Steers puts it, "To give up Booth, Booth would have surely given up Mudd." Which is why, when the authorities questioned Mudd, Mudd played dumb, claiming that he didn't recognize Booth because Booth was wearing a fake beard at the time—lame.

Steers's title alludes to the cliché "his name is mud," erroneously believed to derive from the shame the Lincoln assassination brought to the Mudd family name. But it was simply a coincidence, the derogatory slang "mud" having been in usage for well over a hundred years at the time of the assassination, especially applying to British members of Parliament who had besmirched their family names by losing elections and such. This quirk of freak linguistic happenstance damned the Mudd family to a level of shame unknown to, say, subsequent generations of Family Atzerodt. Meeker folks might have laid low, counting on Americans' amnesia with regards to all things historical to eventually wash away the sins of the father. The Mudds, on the other hand, turned restoring the doctor's good standing into a cottage industry, turning the Mudd farm into a tourist attraction.

Finally, Klam and I find the house, squeaking inside for the last tour of the day. There's another tour guide in period costume. There's another antique store's worth of furniture, some of it, impressively, built by Mudd. This tour is enthralling, partly because the guide is so matter-of-fact. She waves at the bed upstairs, announcing it's the bed where Booth took a nap. In the living room, she nods at the sofa, saying that's where Mudd examined Booth's mangled leg. She's more excited about the piano in the corner, and her excitement is shared. A dark-haired mustachioed man, who bears a slight resemblance to Booth, if Booth wore Bermuda shorts, asks if he can play a song. I'm stunned when the guide lets him in through the velvet rope and the rest of us, including his of course appalled teenage daughter, stand there listening to him bang out a choppy but vaguely familiar tune. After he finishes his song, I ask him, "Sir, were you just playing 'Lean on Me'?"

"That's right!" he answers, thrilled.

Now, whenever I think of Mudd and his house I hear that song, hear Mudd serenading the limping Booth, taking his arm and helping him up the stairs, singing, "Lean on me, when you're not strong, and I'll be your friend."

The Mudd family lived in this house until they sold it to the Maryland Historic Trust in the 1970s. The guide claims there are Mudds everywhere here in Charles County. Many of them help out around the museum. The woman working at the cash register in the gift shop says she's Dr. Mudd's great-great-granddaughter. She's very nice.

The Mudd family project, to redeem the reputation of a relative who's been dead for more than a century, is not without charm. This faith, this love, is understandable, even likable. Actually, I envy the Mudds their faith. This question of questionable ancestors—I've pondered it a lot.

Like my cashier at the Mudd house, I have an historical great-great-grandfather too. And I thought of her great-great-grandfather when I happened to read about the following principle of physics, but mostly I thought about mine. The physics concept is called the "grandfather paradox."

The grandfather paradox poses this riddle: What if a person traveled back in time, encountered her grandfather, got into an argument with the grandfather, and then shot her grandfather to death, thereby ensuring that the granddaughter herself would never be born?

What I like about the grandfather paradox is that it treats time travel not as some lofty exercise in cultural tourism—looking over Melville's shoulder as he wrote *Moby-Dick*—but as a petty excuse to bicker with and gun down one's own relatives.

I just so happen to have a grandfather who deserved it, my great-great-grandfather, John Vowell. The reason why I would set the wayback machine for the sole purpose of rubbing him out is this:

In the 1860s, the teenage John Vowell joined up with pro-slavery guerrilla warrior William Clarke Quantrill, who has been called the "most hated man in the Civil War," which is saying something. On August 21, 1863, Quantrill led his gang, including my great-great-gramps, into Lawrence, Kansas, reportedly ordering them to "kill every male and burn every house." By the end of the day, at least 182 men and boys were dead.

Edward Fitch was shot in his own living room. His widow wrote this letter about witnessing his death: "My dear father and mother, I have been trying to summon strength to write to all the particulars of this sad, sad day . . . which has wrecked all my happiness. Never before did I feel the meaning of the word crushed."

Lawrence was a symbolic target for Quantrill and his men. Since before the Civil War, Lawrence had been the capital of abolitionism in the West. The town had been founded by Free-Soil New Englanders who settled in Kansas to vote to outlaw slavery in the new state. Lawrence had already been sacked once before by a pro-slavery mob in 1856, and in retaliation, the famed abolitionists John Brown and sons attacked a pro-slavery settlement, slaughtering five men as their families looked on. This spawned a grubby little guerrilla war between abolitionist Jayhawkers and the pro-slavery border ruffians of Missouri. Hundreds were killed on both sides in what became known as "Bleeding Kansas," years before the official kickoff of Fort Sumter.

If I were to travel back in time and confront my great-great-grandfather the terrorist, what would we have to say to each other? Remember that in the grandfather paradox, before I kill him, we get into an argument first. Would he defend his motives, tell me some chilling story about the Jayhawker who ruined his life, perhaps enumerate Quantrill's overlooked good qualities? And how might I rebut? Recite "I have a dream"? Sing a few bars of "The KKK Took My Baby Away"? Or maybe I could tell him about the morning in September idealistic young men not unlike himself flew into the city where I live and taught me the meaning of the word crushed.

After my great-great-grandfather and I have it out, let's suppose that against all odds, a gun-toting bushwhacking guerrilla warrior could be overpowered by me, a former art history major. And what am I killing him for? Taking the law into his own hands, murdering people as a political act. This is where my grandfather paradox turns into the grandfather paradox paradox: to prevent my great-great-grandfather from doing wrong, I myself become a vigilante taking justice into my own hands, shooting somebody because I disagree with him. Which is, of course, wrong and exactly what he did.

Curiously, if my great-great-grandfather's friend Quantrill had gotten his way, my cashier, the great-great-granddaughter of Mudd, would not be spending her Saturday selling souvenir coasters depicting the room where Mudd doctored Booth. Legend has it Quantrill rode east in 1865, intending to assassinate President Lincoln. Quantrill was in Kentucky when he heard about Booth. Quantrill got drunk toasting Booth.

Thus do I, descendant of racist, pro-slavery teenage terrorist, buy a copy of *Dr. Samuel A. Mudd Family Home Cooking* from her, descendant of racist, slave-owning, convicted assassination accomplice. It's a cookbook that contains recipes submitted by various Mudd granddaughters and cousins for dishes such as cherry nut bars and three-fruit marmalade.

As Klam drives to the church in Bryantown where Mudd is buried, I page through the cookbook. It says, "Life in the good old days here was centered around the family, hard work, good food and fun games on the plantations and farms." Good old days for everyone but the family slaves.

In *His Name Is Still Mudd,* one of Edward Steers's most powerful, resonant arguments is one that amounts to a tangent. In a curmudgeonly chapter titled "The Good Doctor," Steers turns his attention to Mudd's Hippocratic oath alibi. After enumerating the number of slaves owned by Mudd (eleven), Steers cites the testimony of one of Mudd's former slaves at his conspiracy trial. The slave testified that once, when he was pokey about following Mudd's orders, Mudd shot him, hoping to teach him a lesson about picking up his pace. Then Steers points out that some of the other slaves testified that they were often whipped by Mudd. "By any standard," hisses Steers, "owning slaves and whipping and shooting them seems at variance with the ideals of the Hippocratic oath."

The *Dr. Samuel A. Mudd Family Home Cooking* cookbook says, "In the correspondence with Dr. Mudd while he was imprisoned [at Fort Jefferson in the Dry Tortugas] was mention of the stuffed ham at Easter, the 'gobbler' at Christmas and several references to the Christmas egg nog."

So I booked a ticket for Key West and went to the place where Mudd ate rancid meat if he ate at all, all the while thinking of Christmas turkey, dreaming of Easter ham.

*

I cannot decide whom I resent more, Dr. Mudd or Jimmy Buffett, as I vomit into a paper bag on a boat in the Florida Straits. But as "Margaritaville" thumps on the boat's loudspeaker I am momentarily more famous than the Lincoln assassination conspirator and that laid-back singer-songwriter combined. On today's voyage of the *Yankee Clipper II* I am a celebrity of seasickness, famous on board as the first person to throw up, and then as the person who has thrown up the most. I am famous as the tourist the crew shooed out to the aft railing for "fresh air" and who, after the wind almost blew me overboard, grudgingly chose wanting to die over actually dying, thus ripping open the cabin door in tears screaming,

"I don't like it out there!" I am famous for wedging myself, knuckles white and eyes closed, between the snack bar and the door for an hour and a half, trying to drown out the sound of Jimmy Buffett's voice by softly singing the Beach Boys' "Sloop John B," so that passengers squeezing past me to get to the overhyped fresh air could hear the faint, repeated melody of that song: *This is the worst trip I've ever been on.*

There are only two ways to get from Key West to Fort Jefferson at Dry Tortugas National Park, where Dr. Samuel Mudd and three others convicted for aiding John Wilkes Booth were imprisoned in the 1860s—by boat or seaplane. Except for today: the seaplane pilot, the wise, sane seaplane pilot, canceled my morning flight to the park because of the hazardous wind. Thus am I bobbing up and down here on the edge of the Bermuda Triangle opening up my third paper barf bag to catch what's left of the key lime yogurt I had for breakfast.

It is late autumn here in the Florida Keys, islands where, Hemingway wrote after the 1935 hurricane, "there is no autumn but only a more dangerous summer." (Yesterday, I made the mistake of visiting Hemingway's house in Key West. It was crawling with cats and I'm allergic. So, unable to dodge the sixty-something descendants of Hemingway's six-toed pet, I eyeballed the room where he wrote *Green Hills of Africa* and *For Whom the Bell Tolls* for approximately eight seconds before sneezing back to my hotel room for eye drops and antihistamine.)

After nearly three hours of what the *Yankee Clipper II*'s crew call "cowboying" up and down the bucking waves, Fort Jefferson pops into view. It is an impressive, six-sided brick stronghold built to scare off invaders. I have read Dr. Mudd's letters home describing it as a "godforsaken isle," a "place of woe." I know that a reporter who caught up with Mudd back home in Maryland after his release remarked that in Mudd's "sunken, lusterless eyes, pallid lips and cold, ashy complexion, one can read the words 'Dry Tortugas' with a terrible significance." And yet, right now, for the simple blessed fact that it is not a boat, Fort Jefferson looks as bright and fluffy as a hexagonal lemon meringue pie.

Facts about Dry Tortugas National Park: seventy miles west of Key West; the cluster of islands was discovered by Ponce de Leon in 1513; named the Tortugas, the Spanish word for sea turtles (the adjective "dry" was tacked on later to alert sailors they would drink no fresh water here); Fort Jefferson, named after Thomas Jefferson, was established to protect the shipping lanes to the Gulf of Mexico; it was constructed between 1846 and 1874, when it was abandoned by the United States Army; the fort was never finished, though it was reoccupied by the navy in 1898 thanks to the Spanish-American War; it's ninety miles north of Cuba; in 1861, it became a federal prison; in 1865, the four conspirators convicted of plotting Lincoln's murder who were not hung in Washington were exiled here; three of them—Dr. Samuel A. Mudd, Samuel Arnold, and Ned Spangler—would receive presidential pardons on the last day of Andrew Johnson's administration; the fourth, Michael O'Laughlin, died here during the yellow fever epidemic of 1867; in its heyday, around two thousand people lived here, including a few women and children—mostly officers' families, not to mention the odd laundress (because as punishment imprisoned men were hung up by their thumbs, but apparently a girl job like washing socks was considered cruel and unusual and left to the female hired help); the fort consists of sixteen million bricks shipped at great cost from as far away as Maine; designated by President Franklin Roosevelt a national monument in 1935, the Dry Tortugas became a national park in 1992, offering historical tours, bird-watching, shark research, and snorkeling around its reefs. Also, though this is an island, there is a moat.

Mike Ryan, the interpretative ranger at Dry Tortugas National Park, is waiting on the boat dock. I must look about as healthy as I feel. "Fighting six- to eight-foot seas isn't always that much fun," he sympathizes, leading me across the moat and into the fort for my guided tour.

"This was not an ordinary fort," Mike begins. "It was extraordinarily large."

Inside the brick perimeter is a vast grassy courtyard dotted with palms. There are brick sidewalks and benches shaded by gnarled trees. It's breezy, but peaceful. It is so pleasant I can almost imagine taking a vacation here without the extra tourist glamour of presidential killers and mosquito-borne disease. In fact, most of my fellow passengers are presently pulling on snorkel gear or lining up for the picnic; they will return to the boat hours later with sun-chapped smiles, having gone all day without mentioning yellow fever.

Mike says, "I think it's a paradox that this prison-in-paradise theme's kind of interwoven through. The contrast makes it so compelling."

Guiding me through a brick arcade, Mike stands next to a cannon and points down a corridor. "Some of the views that you'll see today you can't enjoy anywhere else because of these long, unobstructed views looking down wings of archways." He says that the arch motif is repeated a couple of thousand times. The loopy curves soften an otherwise oppressive slab.

"It's pretty funny. They're building arches inside other arches," Mike says of the fort's engineers. "They're kind of showing off if you think about it. In fact, there are many arches you can't see because they're in our foundations." The two thousand arches, not to mention the moat, endow Fort Jefferson with a medieval mood, more William the Conqueror than U. S. Grant.

"The concept is not that different from a castle," Mike agrees. "It shows you how fairly static the technology was. We're still using a castle to protect ourselves. It shows you how unprepared they were for rapid technological changes."

He is referring to the fact that, by the beginning of the Civil War, Fort Jefferson was technologically obsolete. The U.S. government had been shipping brick out here for a couple of decades, trying to build an impregnable fortress with forty-five-foot-high walls that were eight feet thick, until, suddenly, there were steam-powered warships that were no longer at the mercy of wind and were capable of firing rifled artillery that could blow holes straight through the walls.

The War of 1812 witnessed such national security embarrassments as the British burning down the White House, so in the years following, the United States started building coastal forts like this one. Mike declares, "They not only helped prevent war, but they were powerful symbols that we wanted to be left alone. And they fit in very well with the American philosophy at the time. You know, it's only since 1898 that we've become a world power. Prior to 1898, we were very insulated. What better way of insulating ourselves than to build this thick skin?"

Just as technology was compromising Fort Jefferson's usefulness, the Civil War redeemed it. In 1861, Abraham Lincoln designated the fort as a federal prison for Union soldiers, most of them deserters. Lincoln had a soft spot for deserters, whom he called his "legs cases." Though many of his military commanders grumbled about Lincoln's leniency—traditionally, runaways were shot—the president preferred incarceration to execution, asking, "If Almighty God gives a man a cowardly pair of legs how can he help their running away with him?"

That said, Fort Jefferson was harsh. "Bad diet, bad water, and every inconvenience," wrote Mudd to his wife. "Without exception," his cellmate Sam Arnold later recalled, "it was the most horrible place the eye of man ever rested upon, where day after day the miserable existence was being dragged out, intermixed with sickness, bodily suffering, want and pinching hunger, without the additional acts of torture and inhumanity that soon I became a witness of."

Yeah, but how's the food? Arnold described the bread as a "disgusting . . . mixture of flour, bugs, sticks and dirt." He also mentioned that the "meat, whose taint could be traced by its smell from one part of the fort to the other" was so rotten dogs ran away from it, and that the coffee was "slop." As for the accommodations, Arnold portrayed the wall of his cell as "a mass of slime."

The Arnold quotations above are taken from the conspirator's enthralling memoir. Arnold was a recluse for decades after his release from Fort Jefferson. But one day in 1902, he picked up the newspaper and saw his own obituary. Another

Samuel Arnold in a nearby county had died and been mistaken for the friend of Booth. Arnold didn't like what he read. Evidently, helping kill the president gets a guy a surprisingly unflattering obit. So Arnold penned a series of newspaper articles (which were later published as a book) to tell his side of the story.

Mike is a fan of Arnold's writing. It's hard not to be. Arnold described the deprivations of the fort in unflinching detail. For example, he claimed that it was "necessary to dig deep holes and gutters to catch the water, thereby preventing our quarters becoming flooded all over." At the fort, Mike shows me those very gutters. The little circular drainage ditch dug by the conspirators is still there on the floor of an upstairs cell. It's a very dramatic moment, seeing the scrapings of Arnold and Mudd. Pointing my camera at the floor and taking a picture, I can't help but feel for them, how unthinkably demoralizing it must have been, sloshing around standing water that's a better habitat for mosquitoes than men.

The Lincoln conspirators were moved around the fort a few times to different quarters. On the way to showing me another one of their cells, Mike stops in the yard, saying, "This is where they would hang men from their thumbs. Another very popular form of punishment was making men carry cannonballs. Can you imagine a frail man eating a poor diet having to carry a hundred-and-twenty-eight-pound projectile?"

Mike looks down at the green grass, picturing hunched-over cannonball carriers. He says, "They would circle here. They spent two hours on and two hours off, night and day. Depending on the infraction, depending on the whim of the sadistic provost or the officer of the day, this would go on for a couple of weeks. Invariably, the man's not going to survive. He's going to pass out. He's going to collapse." Mike goes on to mention that the civilian family in charge of keeping the lighthouse complained that they couldn't get any sleep at night because of the screams.

We walk past a brown sign announcing "Dr. Mudd's Cell" in a white typeface that fans of geysers and log architecture know and love as the National Park Service font.

Inside, the cell is dark and gloomy. Dried leaves clatter around the concrete floor. Hanging above a doorway is a replica of a sign Mudd knew well, reading, "Whoso entereth here leaveth all hopes behind." It's cribbed from Dante's *Inferno*; these are the words inscribed above the gates to hell.

We entereth anyway. A framed picture of Mudd hangs on the wall.

"Even if you hate Dr. Mudd, you've got to respect what he did during the epidemic," Mike states. In describing the 1867 yellow fever outbreak, the ranger is simultaneously so moved and informed, he speaks in complete paragraphs:

"The army doctor out here died. All four nurses in the hospital died, and that leaves no one but Dr. Mudd. A situation like that takes bravery.

"Four hundred people are living out here at that time— men, women, children, black and white. There were two hundred and seventy cases of yellow fever. That's pretty serious. Thirty-eight died that we know of. Back then, they didn't know what caused yellow fever. They didn't know how to treat it. You would die a very painful death. They called it 'bone fever' or 'break bone fever.' Such intense pain in your joints, in your bones, that you felt like you were going to explode. The latter stages of yellow fever were called 'black vomit,' literally that."

The mention of the black vomit cheers me up. It makes the pale green yogurt I threw up this morning on the boat seem comparatively festive, a thought that causes my mind to momentarily wander to Chicago and fond memories of St. Patrick's Day and kelly-colored beer.

Meanwhile, back at Fort Jefferson, Mike says, "Mudd had some experience treating, or at least attempting to treat, yellow fever in Baltimore, where he apparently worked for a period of time. So he had some background. He understands that perhaps the best thing you can do is keep the victims calm. Often he would sit by their sides, hold their hands, offering comforting words, a cold compress if they were hot, a blanket if they had chills.

"He also understood that they were very susceptible to any kind of stress. What had been a tradition out here was when anyone had yellow fever was to get them off this island, out of Fort Jefferson. There was this small island nearby originally called Sand Key, but they changed the name of it to Hospital Key. It was a hospital in name only. It was really a kind of quarantine. They would take unhealthy inhabitants over there, and oftentimes it was a one-way ticket.

"That island pretty much filled up with dead bodies. There are none there today. Those graves washed away in the hurricane of 1935.

"One thing that Mudd did, even though as a prisoner he had no authority to do this, he said, 'No. No, we're not going to send any more men over to Hospital Key. It's too stressful.' Just the trip alone—you know on a day like today in an open rowboat going about a mile and a half—it's pretty rough! If they survived the trip they're going to be worse than they were when they started. So he made sure all the patients were kept here at the fort.

"The epidemic lasted the better part of two to three months. It essentially ran out of victims. So the deaths just started to decline. But one of those that died was Michael O'Laughlin, one of the Lincoln conspirators."

Hanging on the cell's wall alongside Mudd's photograph is a plaque, from 1961. The plaque quotes Andrew Johnson's pardon, issued on his last day in office, February 8, 1869:

. . . upon occasion of the prevalence of the yellow fever . . . Samuel A. Mudd devoted himself to the care and cure of the sick, and interposed his courage and skill to protect the garrison . . . from peril and alarm, and thus . . . saved many valuable lives and earned the admiration and gratitude of all who observed or experienced his generous and faithful service to humanity.

I am standing there reading the plaque and admiring Mudd—forgiving him.

Mike and I chat about how Mudd had noticed that the epidemic would have been the perfect time to escape, what with the guards laid up with the black vomit, but he resolved to stay and care for the patients. Then Mike asks me, "You know why Mudd tried to escape in September of '65, right?"

Nope.

"Well, it's in a letter. Mudd was quite a, shall we say, white supremacist. You know he was a slave owner. In September of 1865, the U.S. Colored Unit—that's what they called those troops then—arrive at the fort. And Mudd describes this to his wife: 'It is bad enough to be a prisoner in the hands of white men your equals under the Constitution, but to be lorded over by a set of ignorant, prejudiced and irresponsible beings of unbleached humanity, was more than I could submit to.'"

Wincing, Mike continues, "The thought of being guarded by black soldiers was something he felt he could not deal with." So Mudd tried to stow away in a supply ship but was discovered before it left the dock.

Now that I have snapped out of my momentary exoneration of Mudd, I ask Mike if he has formed an opinion regarding Mudd's guilt or innocence in the assassination.

"Out here, of course, we have to be careful. It's prudent to be impartial. Some of our visitors, they come out here—it's like a pilgrimage. They want to see Mudd's cell. They want to talk about this fascinating story. Where else can you do it? You can go to Mudd's home maybe, but that's not really getting to the heart of the matter."

"Yes, they're a little biased there," I agree. Mike smiles at this understatement, knowing as I do that saying they're a little biased in Mudd's favor at the Mudd-family-run Mudd home in Maryland is like saying cheese steaks are kind of associated with Philadelphia.

"So out here we say that we will not resolve guilt or innocence. We simply want to point out what the conditions were like and allow you, whatever your views are, to take that for what it's worth. I do try to point out some things that were brought up in Mudd's trial, how some felt he was simply a country doctor doing his Hippocratic oath. But there was some testimony during the trial that points out that he was probably part of an underground network of Confederate spies. Does that mean he was part of the conspiracy to assassinate the president? Well, probably not. But you know that very damning testimony that Booth had been in his home before?"

"Yes."

"You've been to the home. You couldn't even find it today without roads and signs."

"Yeah," I say. "My friend and I got lost eighteen times and we had MapQuest."

"So imagine if it's three A.M., pitch black. And then what? Booth and Mudd were seen in public together at least twice, right? And in that climate, it was tragic. I mean the first successful assassination. There was so much death and suffering. Mudd could have easily been hanged with that evidence. It's hard to say. He certainly didn't pull the trigger. But I wouldn't be terribly surprised to learn that he may have been part of the plot to kidnap the president. I'm one of the people who believe that if Booth had never broken his ankle, we never would have heard the name Dr. Samuel Mudd."

We go out onto a bastion outside the fort walls to look at the biggest cannon I have ever seen. My father has a thing for cannons, so I ask Mike to take my picture next to it. He says that he ought to take a picture of me inside of it it's so huge.

"It's a fifteen-inch Rodman," he says. "This weighs twenty-five tons. This might come as a surprise, but it's almost the size and the weight of a Sherman tank." The thing can fire a projectile with a diameter of fifteen inches weighing 432 pounds. "Imagine what a four-hundred-and-thirty-two-pound beach ball would do to a wooden sailing ship. This is a nice example of a deterrent."

He adds, "We have six of these cannons, one on top of

SARA H VOWELL

each bastion. This is the largest collection of fifteen-inch Rodmans in existence."

I considered putting an exclamation point at the end of the previous sentence to more accurately portray the gusto with which it was delivered. "This is the largest collection of fifteen-inch Rodmans in existence" doesn't look, on the page, like a sentence full of fun, but it was. Mike's enthusiasm for the fort and what it has to offer is so catching that even when he points his finger at some corroded stretch of brick I get the same giddy feeling I do when leaping into a subway car a split second before the doors close, that feeling of How lucky am I?

He gushes, "There are so many superlatives out here. I've worked in six coastal forts. I've been doing this for about twenty years, and this is arguably the finest coastal fort in the country. And heck, think of all the shipwrecks. We have nearly three hundred shipwrecks in our waters. We have the sooty tern, the birds whose migration is a world treat. People come from around the world to see our spring migration. The turtles, the sharks—some of the most important shark research that's ever been done in the world has been done right out here less than a mile from where we're standing. And this lighthouse," he says, pointing up. "You don't want to forget about lighthouses. This one was built in 1876."

He asks if I'm afraid of heights and would I like to climb the lighthouse. I sigh, telling him that yes of course I'm afraid of heights, not mentioning that of all my phobia (water, driving, snakes, roller coasters, Children of the Corn) and allergies (peanuts, wheat, pet dander, springtime) I'm almost proud of my fear of heights because it seems comparatively ho-hum, sane.

78

To buck myself up for the lighthouse I picture Edward R. Murrow during the Blitz, taking the stairs to that London rooftop. If he can deliver an elegant radio report as the Luftwaffe tried to bomb Big Ben, I shouldn't be such a baby about getting forty feet closer to the occasional migrating bird.

As we ascend the stairs Mike says, "You can hear the wind blowing." Yes, I can. It is the sound of fear.

As Mike unlocks the door he says, "The view's spectacular up here. It's a thousand times better than where we just were. Hold on to your hat, hopefully you won't be blown away."

Well, I am blown away. The view is majestic. Looking out to sea Mike is giddy, cheerfully pointing out which tiny island is Long Key, which one is Bush Key, gesturing toward some whitecaps where Hospital Key used to be, narrating a live-action documentary on the miracle of migration that begins, "The neat thing about a sooty tern . . ."

Then, turning around to look into the interior of the fort, he says, "The only way to really get a perspective on the size and scale of the fort is to come up here. The inside, well, it competes with Yankee Stadium. You could almost say the Roman Colosseum. You could easily fit a dozen football fields with plenty of room. It's just a really big place. And remember it's also a very expensive place, the single most expensive coastal defense fort ever built, and that's part of the reason why. The cost of shipping these bricks out here was sometimes as much as the cost of the bricks themselves. And several ships didn't quite make it. There are wrecks— wrecks upon wrecks—within sight of here. The rationale here is, this would have been a really small city on the sea, kind of like having a really big wall around the middle of the ocean. And remember, you're not only supporting your own remote, very isolated garrison, but you're providing materials—food, gunpowder, even water itself—to the warships that came here. It helps to explain why the engineers considered this one of the most strategic sites in North America. Yes, we're out in the middle of the ocean, yet we're adjacent to the shipping lanes. Roughly speaking, this was the crossroads to the Gulf of Mexico."

He concedes that because of the fort's expense, it was very controversial. He's not saying whether building it was right or wrong.

Then, alluding to current national defense controversies, he says, "Today our brave young men are in Afghanistan and Iraq as part of the same ongoing effort—protecting our freedom, protecting our peace and prosperity, and our way of life. It comes at a huge price."

A current-events lightbulb goes off in my head, one I'd prefer to switch back off. Remembering that little drainage ditch Mudd and Arnold dug into the concrete floor, I turn, looking south. Near here, on the far side of Cuba, more than six hundred prisoners of the War on Terror, a few of them child soldiers under the age of seventeen, are, by executive order, incarcerated at the U.S. base on Guantánamo Bay for who knows how long for who knows what reasons in what Human Rights Watch has called a "legal black hole." Suicide attempts are epidemic. There are rumors of mistreatment—of constant interrogations, sleep deprivation, of inmates chained up in tiny cells. Some of them, maybe even most of them, are, as government spokesmen keep saying, bad people. And that's more or less how I think of Dr.

Mudd—a bad man who did bad things (but happened to be a good doctor). I haven't decided if he deserved to eat bread made out of sticks or live in a rancid puddle, probably because I haven't made up my mind whether anyone deserves such treatment, though I suspect that the day a person gives up on the Geneva Convention is the day a person gives up on the human race. So after I get home from the Dry Tortugas—the nicest thing I can say about the boat ride back to Key West is that I only threw up once—I will click on the Guantánamo link at the Amnesty International Web site and see the headline "Human Rights Scandal" and I will think of Dr. Mudd at Fort Jefferson, digging at the swamp that was his floor.

*

After leaving Dr. Mudd's house, John Wilkes Booth and David Herold pushed south toward Virginia, hiding out in the woods where a Confederate agent named Thomas Jones plied them with food and newspapers. Booth's diary, recovered from his pocket after he died and currently on display in the museum at Ford's Theatre, records the dismay with which the famous actor reacted to his latest reviews. Booth is shocked that what he thought would be regarded as a courageous act of southern patriotism against a despot is covered in the press as the treasonous crime of an evil lunatic. How ungrateful! On April 21, a week after shooting Lincoln, Booth wrote the following in his journal, comparing himself to Brutus, Caesar's assassin immortalized by Shakespeare in the play Booth had performed with his brothers, and William Tell, the Swiss hero who warranted the famous overture for slaying an Austrian bully.

After being hunted like a dog through swamps, woods, and last night being chased by gun boats till I was forced to return wet cold and starving, with every mans hand against me, I am here in despair. And why; For doing what Brutus was honored for, what made Tell a Hero. And yet I for striking down a greater tyrant than they ever knew am looked upon as a common cutthroat. . . . I struck for my country and that alone. A country groaned beneath this tyranny and prayed for this end. Yet now behold the cold hand they extend to me.

Not that I have much sympathy for Booth's groaning, but I think I understand where his befuddlement comes from. Where could Booth have gotten the fantastical idea that committing political murder would be greeted as an act of heroism? Not from the South. I'm pretty sure he got that cockamamie notion from the North. A little poking around in the Booth biography uncovers his earlier rendezvous with history—the 1859 execution of John Brown.

Booth was there in Charles Town, Virginia, witnessing Brown hang. He had been acting in a play in Richmond when he heard that a local militia, the Richmond Grays, was heading north to guard the execution. Like some teenage heavy metal fan worming his way backstage at a Metallica concert, Booth the John Brown fan charmed himself into the Grays' company, bought a uniform, all so he could see his hero breathe his last.

Booth's admiration of Brown was not ideological. Of course, the racist, pro-slavery, future assassin despised the actual cause Brown was fighting for by attacking the federal arsenal at Harper's Ferry—namely, to spark a slave rebellion that would put an end to slavery. But Booth adored Brown's fight-picking, gun-toting methods. According to Booth's sister, Asia, he said, "John Brown was a man inspired, the grandest character of the century!" Booth's assessment was shared, based on the sermons preached in Brown's honor after he died, the church bells that rang in his memory across the North, the tributes written for him by the likes of the revered three-named Yankee poets Ralph Waldo Emerson, Henry David Thoreau, and Julia Ward Howe (who said Brown's martyrdom "would make the gallows glorious like the cross"), the fact that Union soldiers turned the marching song "John Brown's Body" into one of the top-ten hits of the Civil War. So Booth isn't entirely misguided in thinking he'd inspire a song or poem or two himself.

I visited Charles Town with my aunt Fran and uncle Quenton. We found the site where Brown was hanged and Booth stood watch. A fine brick house was built there after the Civil War. The current owner, milling around, invited us into his yard, showed off his stained-glass windows. "They're original Tiffany," he says.

"Imagine that," Aunt Fran whispers. "Tiffany windows looking out on the place where John Brown was hanged."

The owner pointed at a tree on his lawn. "That's where the gallows were." A bird feeder is suspended on a limb of the tree, swaying back and forth where Brown's neck swung. (It reminds me of North Elba, New York, where Brown is buried. Looming over Brown's humble little farm is the mondo ski jump from the Lake Placid Olympics. A person going there to ponder the dour Brown can end up thinking a lot more about how much she misses the voice of sportscaster Howard Cosell.)

From Charles Town, Fran and Quenton drive me to D.C., dropping me off at my hotel, the Washington Hilton. Later, I'll read the caption on a postcard in my room with a photo of the brutalist white building. It boasts, "Curved at every point, the hotel is shaped like a seagull in flight." It reminds me more of a spatula about to scrape a bowl. Then there's a list of all the reasons a person should want to stay here—shuffleboard for instance—but no mention of the reason I want to. This is where Hinckley shot Reagan in 1981.

Because of the news footage of the shooting, I've seen that bowed rock wall in the driveway, heard the shots hundreds of times. And looking at it I feel reverent, though not so much about Reagan, partly because he's a person I find difficult to revere, but mostly because of the cheery way he yukked it up during his recovery. Not that I blame him. Just as he cracked to the doctors who were saving his life that he hoped they were all Republicans, the one time I came to in an ambulance (following a bike accident in which I hit a parked car) was during Reagan's successor's administration. The medic asked me who the president was and I answered, "George Bush, but I didn't vote for him." It pains me that, like Reagan, faced with the profundity of death my first conscious impulse was to act like a smart-alecky partisan jackass.

The reason I well up with liturgical emotion on seeing that entrance to the Hilton is not because Reagan was attacked here, but because his press secretary, James Brady, was. That Brady will spend the rest of his life in a wheelchair is cause enough for empathy. That he and his wife, Sarah, turned this rotten luck into the Brady Campaign to Prevent Gun Violence is downright heroic. And not the soft-focus treacle that "heroic" often implies. I'm on their mailing list, and the most impressive, lovable thing about them is their rage. The last mailing I got, seeking help to close the gun show loophole laws that allow terrorists and criminals to purchase all the firearms they want as long as it's at folding tables set up at fairgrounds, featured a letter from Jim that opens, "I'm sitting here in my wheelchair today, mad as hell, trying to control my anger," and another one from Sarah in which she tells a story about how right after Jim was shot, her son was playing with what he thought was a toy gun in a family member's truck, but it turned out to be real and when she learned this she stormed over to the phone and called up the National Rifle Association, telling them, "This is Sarah Brady and I want you to know that I will be making it my life's work to put you out of business!" Unbelievably, two years after the assassination attempt President Reagan addressed the NRA's national convention—the only sitting president ever to do so. Who should have known more than he that backing an organization lobbying against (especially) the control of handguns is against the self-interest of every president. After all, only John F. Kennedy was shot with a rifle; the other three successful presidential murders (and the attempted assassinations of Theodore and Franklin Roosevelt, Harry Truman, and Gerald Ford) were committed with handguns. In fact, Booth's dainty derringer is on display across town in the Lincoln Museum at Ford's Theatre. It's downright pretty until you remember the damage it did.

The next morning, Klam arrives in the driveway where Reagan's car had been waiting. We're going to pick up where we left off on the John Wilkes Booth escape route tour. We're heading to the spot where Booth died.

Not far from Port Royal, Virginia, there's a sign. It reads,

"This is the Garrett Place where John Wilkes Booth, Assassin of Lincoln, was cornered by Union soldiers and killed, April 26, 1865. The house stood a short distance from this spot."

Booth's sidekick David Herold surrendered to the soldiers, so he would live to hang. Booth, however, holed up in the barn with a gun, refusing to come out. So the soldiers lit it on fire. There are conflicting reports about who fired on Booth—soldier Boston Corbett or a suicidal Booth himself—but shot, he staggered from the barn and lived long enough to die in Garrett's living room. His last words, also in dispute, might have been "Tell my mother I died for my country."

It was here Booth's body was wrapped up in a horse blanket to be taken back to Washington, where his autopsy would be performed. Surgeon General Joseph K. Barnes, after inspecting Booth's corpse, ended his report, "Paralysis of the entire body was immediate, and all the horrors of consciousness of suffering and death must have been present to the assassin during the two hours he lingered." Subtext: You'll be happy to know he really suffered.

Klam and I get out of the car and poke around on the side of the road. It's scratchy, full of brambles, fallen logs, and yellow leaves. We can't get far, not that we want to. After Klam kicks around an historic plastic bottle of Sprite, we head back to the car. That's when he notices another sign, a mysterious pictograph of a hand with a finger pointing across the road.

Following the finger, we come to a small, peaceful clearing. It's on a wide wooded median between Route 301N and 301S. There, at eye level, hanging above a wreath tied with a black ribbon on an ornate iron gate is a photograph encased in plastic: a mustachioed head shot of John Wilkes Booth. Back in art school we would have called this setup an installation. What it really is is a shrine, a lovely, symmetrical, classical shrine. Two Roman-looking black planters of evergreen trees stand next to two Roman-looking concrete benches. It would be the perfect picnic spot as long as you're fine with eating under Booth's smoldering stare.

I step up to Booth's photo, yanking it off its perch to get a closer look. I'm so startled by the place that I accidentally drop it on the ground.

"Careful," says Klam. "That's a hundred-thousand-dollar fine."

He gestures at a sign prohibiting the "disturbance of artifacts from these lands."

Down the road, in Port Royal, we stop for breakfast at a roadside diner cum gas station where we experience both the best (ham and grits) and the worst (Confederate flag crap) the South has to offer. After I polish off my grits I examine the Confederate flag memorabilia for sale—the shot glasses, the baseball caps, "Never Surrender" mugs. I am enthralled with a hideous, huge music box/snow globe of Robert E. Lee that plays "Dixie" when you wind it. I consider adding it to my snow globe collection, but that would involve having it in my house.

We are near the battlefield at Fredericksburg. I'm going to give this place the benefit of the doubt and decide that that's why all this stuff's here and not the proximity to the John Wilkes Booth shrine. However, displayed right alongside all the Confederate flag paraphernalia is a bunch of American flag merch—American flag place mats, patriotic "body crystals," flag stickers you attach to your skin. Personally, I'm small-minded and literal enough that I see the two symbols as contradictory, especially in a time of war. But I fear that the consumer who buys a Confederate flag coffee cup, which she will then put on her American flag place mat, is the sort of sophisticated thinker who is open-minded enough that she is capable of hating blacks *and* Arabs at the same time.

Which brings me to the creepiest thing about Booth's death spot—the sign. The signs were erected by the state of Virginia. Logically, they bear the state's official seal. And that seal of course features the state motto, inscribed in Latin: *Sic semper tyrannis.* It is unfair of me to say so, but the slogan Booth shouted from the stage of Ford's Theatre, the over-blown, self-important, pseudo-Shakespearean blather, being etched on the sign marking his death feels like the stamp of approval.

Klam and I pass other *Sic semper*ed signs on the way back to D.C., most of them devoted to the Civil War. I just sigh, happy that, unlike John Wilkes Booth, we get to get the hell out of here alive, driving toward what my favorite state slo-gan, that of Seward's beloved Alaska, proclaims: North to the Future.

*

"Is Baltimore made up entirely of slums?" my friend Brent asks on the road to Green Mount Cemetery, where John Wilkes Booth is buried. Entire blocks go by with nary a win-dow intact. All the glass is cracked, smashed, or has been re-placed with makeshift plywood. Tired-looking men and women loiter on stoops, the sidewalks piled with trash.

Whereas the living of Baltimore could use a renovation, the dead rest in resplendent peace. Green Mount is one of those pastoral nineteenth-century graveyards inspired by Mount Auburn in Cambridge. Edwin Booth is actually buried there in Massachusetts alongside his first wife, but the rest of the Booths rest here in the Baltimore family plot.

Brent, slowly navigating the car around the graveyard's narrow curves, calls the layout "a Candy Land of death." I locate the Booths by consulting a book on local cemeteries entitled *The Very Quiet Baltimoreans*.

The white obelisk in honor of the patriarch, Junius Brutus Booth, also features an inscription in memory of his children. John Wilkes makes this list, along with his brothers and sisters, but his actual grave here is unmarked.

Brent sits down on the grass. He's wearing a T-shirt from the Emma Goldman Papers Project, an archive of the anarchist's writings at UC Berkeley. The shirt says, "Out of the chaos the future emerges in harmony and beauty." (What poppycock.) He listens quietly as I tell him about John Wilkes Booth. When I get to the assassination part, mentioning Booth's cry of *Sic semper tyrannis,* he asks what that means.

"Thus always to tyrants," I say.

"I wore the wrong shirt then! My other Emma Goldman shirt says 'Woe to tyrants!' "

It is interesting how, once one edits justifications for violence down to a length suitable for T-shirt slogans, political distinctions between left and right disappear. Emma Goldman, anarchist Russian Jewish advocate of free love and birth control sounds exactly like pretty boy white supremacist murderer John Wilkes Booth. Which, come to think of it, isn't that surprising since Goldman, like Booth, was also a vocal member of the John Brown fan club.

I tell Brent that in 1869, Wilkes Booth's mother, sister, and brother Edwin petitioned President Andrew Johnson to have their relative's body returned to them. The family, minus Edwin, held a secret funeral here. Some far-fetched accounts even say that when they went to view Wilkes's body at the mortician's, they passed around his decapitated head. According to *The Very Quiet Baltimoreans*, "Rector Fleming James of St. Mark's Protestant Episcopal Church on Lombard Street attended [the funeral]. He was later placed under 'ban of his church for having officiated at the burial of Lincoln's assassin.' "

A flock of black crows swoops in, landing on the tombstones and the trees, making a racket. We have Edgar Allan Poe on the brain, having stopped at his grave in another cemetery across town before coming here. Looking at the birds reminiscent of the raven Poe wrote his famous poem about flitting around the grave of John Wilkes Booth reminds me how much the two Marylanders have in common. Besides the fact that they looked alike with their dark hair, dark eyes, and dark moustaches, they were both the sons of actors who spent significant parts of their careers in the southern capital of Richmond—Poe editing the *Southern Literary Messenger* magazine, Booth performing in its theaters. Booth died as a result of shooting the president; Poe died—of what root cause, no one knows for sure, though possibilities include rabies, carbon monoxide poisoning, and dipsomania—at the end of a snowy Election Day, found slumped over in a polling place, probably because he had been hired as a "repeater," i.e., a money-grubbing wretch who is paid to go from one poll to another voting again and again. In other words, both Booth and Poe died thwarting the will of the electorate.

Out of fairness, I should mention the generations of conspiracy theorists who believe that John Wilkes Booth is not buried here at Green Mount. But really, I bring up the following story for one reason and it has nothing to do with fairness. I'm in it for the mummy.

Suppose, the story goes, Booth, in collusion with the Andrew Johnson government, escaped from Virginia and someone else was killed, and thus buried in his place. He traveled west, assuming the alias John St. Helen, where, in frontier Texas, he confessed his true identity to a local lawyer, Finis L. Bates, who defended him in 1872 against charges of selling whiskey and tobacco without a license. Booth a.k.a. St. Helen felt free to reveal his real name thanks to the code of silence that is the attorney-client privilege. St. Helen eventually moved away, and Bates never heard from him again. But in 1903, Bates spotted a newspaper article reporting that a man named David E. George had committed suicide in Enid, Oklahoma. Before he died, George confessed that he was John Wilkes Booth. Bates made a beeline for Enid and saw the body, claiming that though twenty-five years had gone by, he recognized George as St. Helen.

George's body was then mummified. Surprise, surprise, the academic record on a mummy made out of an Okie suicide thought to be John Wilkes Booth turns out to be rather dodgy. Whether Bates bought the body and had it mummified, or whether it was the Enid undertaker, someone toured a Booth mummy around in carnivals and freak shows for decades. The mummy's whereabouts are currently unknown.

Still, the legend of David E. George, to say nothing of the mummy sightings, inspired a group, including John Wilkes Booth's great-great-grandniece and his first cousin twice removed, to petition the Baltimore City Circuit Court in 1995 to exhume the body buried at Green Mount in order to identify it. The judge denied the request, partly because of the strong historical evidence that Booth has been buried at Green Mount all along, and partly because his precise location in the Booth family plot is unknown, so that exhuming him would involve a lot of distasteful digging up of everyone in the vicinity. The petitioners appealed the judge's decision but they were denied.

*

The collection of the Mütter Museum in Philadelphia includes a number of attention grabbers. There is a skeleton (deformed from "overzealous corset-wearing"), a wax model of a small pox–infected arm polka-dotted with pustules, a deceased obese woman whose ample fat morphed postmortem into a waxy blob (thus earning her the nickname "the soap lady"), a display case full of old skulls, the two-man plaster cast made during the autopsy of conjoined twins Chang and Eng, and the "mega colon." But I'm here to look at this thing floating in a glass jar labeled "Piece of John Wilkes Booth, Assassin of President Lincoln."

Beige and bloated, the Booth bit resembles a crumpled paper towel. It is part of an exhibit called "When the President is the Patient." It sits among displays devoted to Lyndon Johnson's gallbladder surgery; Grover Cleveland's secret operation to remove a cancerous growth from his cheek that took place on board a yacht in Long Island Sound; a copy of the Twenty-fifth Amendment to the Constitution (ratified in 1967 in the wake of the Kennedy assassination) outlining presidential succession due to incapacity, resignation, or death; photographs of aging white men in shorts labeled "President Carter Jogging" and "President Clinton Jogging"; and, interestingly, another jar with another wadded-up looking item identified as "Portions of the brain of Charles Guiteau, Assassin of President Garfield."

The Mütter Museum is a thing of beauty, a cozy, old-fashioned throwback. Its polished wood curiosity cabinets are clues to its origins. Founded in 1856 when Thomas Dent Mütter, a professor of surgery, donated his collection of medical specimens to the College of Physicians of Philadelphia, the museum's mission was educational, to help med students and practicing doctors learn about disease and thus its treatment.

I took the train to Philadelphia from New York to see the museum, especially the specimens of Booth and Guiteau, and to talk to the museum's director, Gretchen Worden. Dressed in a smart black suit, she's more glamorous than I expected. She reminds me of Ava Gardner, if Ava Gardner happened to keep a book on her desk about the history of diabetes as illustrated in international postage stamps.

We had scheduled our meeting on the only day in October both of us were free. It wasn't until I had boarded the train and opened the newspaper that I fully comprehended the date, October 31. I was going to a musty old house of skulls and things floating in jars on Halloween. So I asked Worden if every day is Halloween at the museum.

"No, no day is Halloween here. I always say it's really about All Saint's Day. It's really about tomorrow, about when we give thanks to those people who have died before and for everything that they have done for us. And in this case, it's people whose bodies or body parts are here in the museum who have made possible the education of physicians, whether it's a willing or unwitting contribution. That I think is a way we ought to look at the collections and not just think of it as all spooky and weird. It has nothing to do with spooky and weird. It really does make people think we're macabre, and I keep saying, 'We're not about death, we're about life.' We're about what was necessary to teach a physician how to keep someone alive."

"Maybe for you then every day is Memorial Day?"

"Yes."

I ask how the museum came into possession of its Booth specimen.

"All we know is the information we have on the label," Worden answers. "It says, 'Sent by a messenger of the Surgeon General.' The surgeon general at the time was Joseph K. Barnes. The only information on it was this old label that said, 'Piece of the thorax of John Wilkes Booth.' And for years we had no reason to question it because we never did any research into it. And it was only when I was finally trying to figure out what piece that was that I realized they didn't do but a routine autopsy on him. So there's no way it could come from the thorax."

She continues, "For years, because of the political associations with Booth, his specimens were hidden away in a tin in a drawer until the curator found it."

"When was it found?"

"Maybe in the thirties or forties. By then, the feelings had changed. There was not that sense of immediate revulsion against John Wilkes Booth that there had been in 1865. So they put out an exhibit. And I have it right now up in my presidential assassination part of the presidential health exhibit. We used to have it downstairs where the mega colon is. I had Chief Justice Marshall's bladder stones in one half of a case and I had John Wilkes in the other. It was simply as a historical specimen of interest because of the association. I didn't tie it in to the whole story as we do up there now. The reason why? One, it's really an interesting thing just to look at something and think, 'Oh, there's a piece of John Wilkes.' And the other is that potentially all of this material is valuable whether it's an anonymous ovarian cyst or a piece of John Wilkes, for the information we might be able to get from it should we choose to go and do DNA testing."

This is especially true for the Garfield assassin Guiteau's brain. "It was suggested at one point that he might be suffering from neurosyphilis," she says. "At the time they really didn't have good ways of examining tissue, or proving it. We now do. Having the tissue allows you to go back in and ask new questions of old specimens."

I mention that I was disappointed that the Mütter's Booth and Guiteau specimens don't show up on FindAGrave.com. Worden has never heard of my favorite Web site. A database listing the names, brief biographies, and burial locations of more than twenty thousand historical figures, one of its curious features is that, usually, if a dead person's body parts are buried in more than one location, all known locations are given. For example, Abraham Lincoln's page of course cites his Springfield tomb, but it also points the reader to Lincoln's skull fragments on display at Washington's National Museum of Health and Medicine.

While I was telling her all that, Worden has wheeled over to her computer and called up the site. Seeing the space to type in a subject's first and last name she types in "John Brown," explaining that she had just returned from Harper's Ferry.

"Me too," I say, launching into my theory about John Wilkes Booth crouching in the pine thicket after the Lincoln assassination, mortified that the papers are calling him an evil lunatic, when he thought he was going to be praised and worshiped like the abolitionists' favorite murderer, John Brown.

She sighs, murmuring, "I really feel sorry for John Wilkes."

"You do?"

"After reading his account of being hunted by dogs, of being so surprised by the reaction to what he had done. Plus, he's so cute."

"Really cute," I agree.

"He was a sorry figure. He just didn't get the big picture. God knows he was not the only one that would have shot Lincoln."

That's true.

"See," she continues. "We've made a myth out of Lincoln. So people are very surprised to find out that anyone could hate this saint, and you look back at the time and John was just one of many. Though the fact is, he just made some really, really bad decisions."

"Yeah," I laugh.

Booth's, she says, "was not a happy death. It was certainly a slower one. At least he was awake while he was dying."

I gingerly pose a personal question, informing her she doesn't have to answer it if she doesn't want to, but I'm curi-

ASSASSINATION VACATION

ous about how working here—and she has worked at the Mütter Museum for nearly thirty years—has affected the way she thinks about her own death and what will happen to her body after she dies.

"I'm still debating," she says, delighted to be asked, "how I want my body to be preserved in the museum."

Stupidly, I think I had meant did she want to be buried or cremated. "In the museum?" I repeat.

"Oh, absolutely. That's traditional. A lot of the curators end up as part of their collections. You know Jeremy Bentham?"

Can't say I do.

"Eighteenth-century Englishman. He was associated with the University of London. He had his body mummified with the stipulation in his will that he shall attend all of the annual meetings. So they keep his body in the closet and then they have to wheel him out."

"Still?"

"Yes, they do it. I mean now his face is missing; it's modeled in wax, but it's still this skeleton with clothes on it. It's very cool. There are others. Loren Eiseley, the great scientist, donated himself to the University of Pennsylvania, but he didn't want to be the 'skeleton of Loren Eiseley.' He wanted to be just one in the anatomical collections that the students would use routinely for studying—very modest man. But now there are so many more possibilities: freeze-drying, which makes you pretty light"—pretty crunchy too I think, remembering the freeze-dried strawberries I had sprinkled on my breakfast yogurt—"or plastination; more flexibility. It's always fun joking about it, but basically the coolest thing would be to have some sort of ironclad will where I have to attend every senior staff meeting to eternity and where I have a permanent display just to make myself as big a pain in the neck to every future curator. If I apply the same criteria to myself that I apply to other people who want to donate their bodies or parts, I really have to come up with something that's going to be educational, whether it's pathology or an interest in anatomy, and I don't know that I can justify my obsession."

"Don't sell yourself short. You might get some really rare disease."

"I'm working on it. It would be nice to be part of this place. It's already gotten my blood, tears, and sweat."

"Might as well get the rest of you?"

"Yeah."

I mention that I used to go to the School of the Art Institute of Chicago and that the museum's collection includes John the Baptist's tooth. The tooth is housed in a reliquary. And though that reliquary was prettier and more elaborate than the simple, scientific glass jars housing the chips off Messrs. Booth and Guiteau, the effect of looking at the objects was the same. What, I ask, is the difference between a relic and a specimen?

"It depends on the specimen," she says. "We do have some pieces of famous people, but the other specimens are simply important because they are demonstrating a particular pathology or anatomy that we want to show. So it varies. But the importance of the relic, the importance of the little sacred icon, is a sense of connection to the past. To look on a tooth, look at George Washington's teeth, to look at instruments that were actually handled by Joseph Lister, there's power in there.

"I still have some of my mother's clothes, you know, for no other reason than I can't bear to part with them. Because it's her favorite sweater, stuff like that. Because of the fact that it was an immediate contact with somebody it just brings up memories. It's also interesting. If you want to know that Joseph Lister used this particular instrument and we have a set, that provides you more information about his practice of medicine, etc. But often it's simply the almost sentimental association of the fact that this is a piece of a great man. It's the same thing as a piece of the true cross."

The way she lumps in Joseph Lister, the pioneer of antiseptic surgery, with her mother makes me wonder if she thinks of the specimens in the museum as her friends.

"No," she grins. "They're like my bosses."

*

Back home in New York, I'm always bumping into John Wilkes Booth's big brother, Edwin. I see Edwin's statue almost every day. He's so familiar and homey I would almost consider him my mascot but for the fact that he's fenced off in Gramercy Park and I am one of the 7,999,900 New Yorkers who do not have a key. It's the only private park in New York, and to get in, you either have to live in one of the lovely brick and brownstone buildings on the park's perimeter or you have to play bass guitar in one of the bands that are always staying at the Gramercy Park Hotel.

The neighborhood of Gramercy Park, where Edwin used to live, was built to look like London, which is to say that its considerable beauty is skin deep while its heart beats with the ugliness of monarchy. And at its very center, inside the gates keeping out the riffraff that is all New York, stands the statue of the sad and fancy Edwin Booth, dressed as Hamlet, his signature role.

I like Edwin. I'm fond of Shakespeare too, but mostly because of the way I grew up watching his plays—sitting in the Montana dirt. In my home state, there was Shakespeare every summer put on by a heroic organization called Shakespeare in the Parks—parks, by the way, with no fences around them, parks a citizen can walk in and out of any damn time she wants.

I live six blocks down Twenty-first Street from Gramercy Park and even though I walk by it every other day, I have been inside it precisely once, when my friend Nick, a Londoner, came to town and stayed at the Gramercy Park Hotel. How fitting that I cannot enter a park on my street without the escort of a subject of the British crown.

Nick gets the hotel's bellman to unlock the gate for us. Then the bellman asks how long we would like to stay. Why does he care? Because he has to know when to come back and *un*lock the gate. Unbelievable.

Nick seems to like the park, but then he likes anyplace in America where he can smoke. We mosey toward Edwin's behind. A life-size bronze in Elizabethan garb, his head's bowed, as if he's about to ask Hamlet's that-is-the-question question. Like the Prince of Denmark, Edwin could have come up with at least three reasons not to be. For starters, little brother going down in history as the president's killer was a cringing, galling shame. Before that, as a boy on the road with his drunken actor father, Junius Brutus Booth, when Edwin finally chose his own stage career over being Junius's babysitter, the elder Booth only lasted a few days without him, drinking rancid river water and dying, sick, on the Mississippi. Though it's hard to blame a kid for wanting more out of life than holding back his father's hair every night as he vomited up his Shakespearean pay, Edwin felt responsible for Junius's demise. Not that this guilt kept Edwin off the bottle. When Mary, his first and favorite wife, was lying on her deathbed in Boston, Edwin was in New York, too smashed to make the last train north. She was dead when he got there. He kicked himself for the rest of his life.

"So who was he?" Nick asks, pointing at Edwin's statue.

"Only the greatest Shakespearean actor of the nineteenth century."

Says the English accent, "You mean, in America?"

Whatever. I let that slide. I've been dying to get inside this park for years, but eventually, I'm going to need Nick and his bellman to get me out.

I tell him how Edwin was known as *the* Hamlet of his day; how his father, Junius Brutus was the greatest Shakespearean actor in England, until 1821, when he emigrated to Maryland, at which point he became the greatest Shakespearean actor in America; how three of Junius's children became actors themselves—Edwin, John Wilkes, and Junius Brutus Jr.; how the three brothers appeared onstage together only once, in *Julius Caesar* here in New York in 1864 as a benefit performance for the Shakespeare statue in Central Park; how their performance was interrupted because that was the night that Confederate terrorists set fires in hotels up and down Broadway and Edwin, who was playing Brutus, interrupted the play to reassure the audience; how the next morning Edwin informed John at breakfast that he had voted for Lincoln's reelection and they got into one of the arguments they were always having about North versus South;

how Edwin retired from acting out of shame when he heard his brother was the president's assassin, but that nine months later, broke, he returned to the stage here in New York, as Hamlet, to a standing ovation; how he bought the house on Gramercy Park South and turned it into the Players Club, a social club for his fellow thespians and others, including Mark Twain and General Sherman; how he built his own theater, the Booth, on Twenty-third and Sixth, where Sarah Bernhardt made her American debut; and how, in the middle of the Civil War, on a train platform in Jersey City, he rescued a young man who had fallen onto the tracks and that man was Robert Todd Lincoln, the president's son, so he's the Booth who saved a Lincoln's life.

It is remarkable that Edwin earned back the public's affection after his brother had committed such a crime. It says something about his talent and his poise that he could pull this off. I have a recording of Edwin, performing Othello, from an 1890 wax cylinder. It sounds like a voice from the grave, so thick with static the only phrase I can understand is "little shall I." Though I cannot make out most of the words, something of Edwin's gentleness comes across, a kind of wispy melancholy I can imagine inspiring more sympathy than scorn.

Perhaps this is the approach Dr. Mudd's grandson Richard should have taken. Instead of spending his very long life pestering state legislatures to pass resolutions recognizing his grandfather's innocence, if he really wanted to get the country behind his family name, he should have recorded a hit song or come up with a dance craze or something.

In Bel Air, the Booths' hometown in Maryland, Edwin is a local hero. The Edwin Booth Memorial Fountain stands in front of the courthouse, next to a sign announcing that Edwin made his theatrical debut in the building. A WPA mural in the post office depicts the scene: a gangly teenager in tails leans pompously toward the assembled audience, half of whom have their heads in their hands they look so bored. A roadside historical marker at Tudor Hall reads, "The home of the noted actor Junius Brutus Booth, the Elder. Birthplace of his children. His son Edwin Booth was born here November 13, 1833." That's the whole sign. No mention of John Wilkes unless you count that cryptic reference to "his children."

Edwin's Players Club still exists in Gramercy Park. It remains the club Edwin envisioned, a fancy place for actors and their friends to get together. Edwin, the illegitimate son of a drunk, the heartbroken brother of an assassin, longed for propriety and elegance. He was an actor back when theater was one of the trashier professions. His actor brother offing the president in a theater didn't improve his profession's profile. Thus did Edwin establish the Players. It's a beautiful house. I've been inside a few times, mostly for literary events. The last time I went, after wandering around and admiring the Edwin memorabilia on display—the John Singer Sargent portrait of Edwin hanging over the fireplace, the helmet he wore as Brutus in *Julius Caesar*—I listened to a novelist confess that his childhood sexual awakening occurred while watching a Porky Pig cartoon in which Porky dressed up in high heels.

Edwin would have loved his statue in Gramercy Park— the first statue of an actor in the city. He warranted a stained-glass window too—a multicolored Shakespearean portrait in the Church of the Transfiguration on Twenty-ninth. Known as the Little Church Around the Corner, it became an actors' church in the nineteenth century because it was the one church in town where actors would be granted a proper funeral.

The church hosted Edwin's funeral on June 9, 1893. Just as his pallbearers were carrying his coffin out the door in New York, in Washington, three floors of Ford's Theatre collapsed. The building had been turned into a government office building after the Lincoln assassination. Twenty-two federal employees died.

*

"In this room, the last of Abraham Lincoln's fourteen funerals took place," says the tour guide upstairs at the Old State Capitol building. "At eight o'clock on May third, 1865, after making eleven stops, Lincoln's funeral train arrived here in Springfield. An honor guard escorted his casket to this room."

The guide, who has a white beard and wears glasses on a chain around his neck, has shown us—and by us I mean uniformed seventh graders on a field trip from their all-girls school in Chicago and me—into the semicircular former chamber of the Illinois House of Representatives, which was, he claims, "the biggest room in the state of Illinois in 1839."

A platform, he says, was built under the painting of George Washington to hold Lincoln's casket. It was here under the Washington portrait's gaze that the future president delivered his "House divided" speech in 1858, famously prophesizing that "this government cannot endure, permanently half slave and half free," unaware that he would be the man to fulfill this prophecy, that he would be the man who made the government "all one thing, or all the other," and that for his trouble he would be murdered only to end up here, again beneath this portrait, a corpse. "In twenty-four hours, seventy-five thousand people came to pay their respects. The population of Springfield at that time was only sixteen thousand seven hundred."

The tour guide has an overly generous idea of the school-girls' knowledge of history because he keeps quizzing them and patiently waiting out interminably awkward silences for answers that never come. In the Senate chamber, he shows them a painting of a dashing old man in a fur coat who looks like Oscar Wilde as played by Gerard Depardieu. The guide wants the girls to guess the gent's identity, dropping loads of clues about how he's French and he served in the Revolutionary War and HE'S FROM FRANCE. It's a relief when the guide finally gives up, shouting, "Marquis de Lafayette!"

I am invariably the odd man out on tours like this. The only people who take them are kids who are forced to endure them and elderly retirees. I am always either the oldest person on a tour, or the youngest. I prefer to be the youngest if only because usually that means I'm the prettiest by default. (Before coming here to the capitol I had already dropped in for the tour at Lincoln's law office, a place overrun by nineteen very mature Ohioans, one of whom told me that they were having a reunion here in Springfield, a reunion commemorating a caravan they all took to Alaska sixteen years ago. That's how very old they are—old enough to have been taking trips like this for sixteen years. They make no comments about the horsehair sofa with a copy of the *New York Tribune* strewn over it to suggest a lounging Lincoln lying there reading aloud or the kind of upside-down top hat the disorganized lawyer is said to have used as his only filing cabinet, but they have plenty to say about having to go up and down stairs, concluding that "it's sure easier going down.")

In the Old State Capitol, one of the seventh graders points to a brassy object, asking the tour guide, "What's that big bowl?" The guide, shocked, answers, "That's a cuspidor, a spittoon." I can understand how these kids might not have heard of Lafayette, but is it possible they have never seen a single episode of *Gunsmoke*?

By the time we arrive at the statue of Lincoln's old debating partner (and possible rival for the hand of Mary Todd), Senator Stephen Douglas, the guide demands the Chicago kids tell him Douglas's nickname. Clearly, they don't even know Douglas's actual name so, a little impatient to get out of here, I can't stop myself from blurting out, "Little Giant. They called him the Little Giant." One of the kids looks at me, then at the diminutive statue of Douglas, who was five foot three. She raises her hand and wants to know why someone so short would be called a giant. To which the guide, exasperated, mumbles, "Well, he was a giant in *politics*."

*

Lincoln's tomb in Springfield's Oak Ridge Cemetery is a towering white obelisk plopped on top of a crypt of marble corridors decorated with bronze tablets of his best-loved speeches and reproductions of the greatest hits of Lincoln statuary, including the seated Lincoln sculpture by Daniel Chester French in Washington's Lincoln Memorial, the August Saint-Gaudens in Chicago's Lincoln Park. It's all a little busy, overly chockablock.

The remains of Mary Todd Lincoln, as well as those of their sons Tad, Willie, and Eddie, are buried in the tomb. There's also an inscription for the oldest son, Robert Todd Lincoln, noting that he's buried at Arlington National Cemetery. (There's a story as to why—supposedly, his widow couldn't stand the thought of her husband, and eventually herself, spending all of eternity next to her dreaded mother-in-law—but of course that's not brought up here.)

What looks like Lincoln's tomb is surrounded by flags and inscribed in gold letters with Secretary of War Stanton's deathbed proclamation, "Now he belongs to the ages." Actually, the president is buried below, under ten feet of concrete. His son Robert, who became a lawyer for the Pullman Palace Car Company, witnessed the burial arrangements of his boss, George Pullman, a man so loathed by his formerly striking workers that he had himself buried under cement and steel so as to prevent the desecration of his grave. Robert was always worried about the security of his father's tomb, especially after the Secret Service had thwarted a grave-robbing plot in 1876 when a counterfeiting gang cooked up a plan to steal Abraham Lincoln's remains and hold them for ransom in exchange for the release of their imprisoned engraver. Robert liked Pullman's approach and shelled out seven hundred dollars to pour concrete on top of his dad.

The Museum of Funeral Customs is on the edge of Oak Ridge Cemetery, a five-minute walk from the tomb. Supposedly the fellow who swoops over to greet me is the museum director, but he speaks in the hushed low voice of a funeral director. He warns me about "the sensitive nature of our exhibits."

Please. I actually giggle when he tries to steel me for seeing the re-created 1920s embalming room, as if I'm not wearing Bela Lugosi hair clips; as if I didn't just buy a book for my nephew called *Frankenstein and Dracula Are Friends*; as if I was never nicknamed Wednesday (as in Addams); as if in eighth-grade English class, assigned to act out a scene from a biography, when all the other girls had chosen Queen Elizabeth or Anne Frank, I hadn't picked Al Capone and staged the St. Valentine's Day Massacre with toy machine guns and wadded-up red construction paper thrown everywhere to signify blood; as if I'm not here to see the replica of Abraham Lincoln's casket; as if I'm not the kind of person who would visit the freaking Museum of Funeral Customs in the first place.

Lincoln's walnut casket was "covered in broadcloth and adorned with silver studs." Black, it has a white satin interior and white fringe. It's also decorated with silver stars. The effect is startling. The only word I can think of to describe it is "snazzy." It has a country-and-western showbiz quality, reminding me of the shiny rhinestone-studded suits Nashville singers used to wear to the Grand Ole Opry.

I stand there and read a very interesting brochure entitled *The Embalming of President Lincoln*. It makes note of the fact that the Lincoln funeral train was the best advertising the nascent embalming industry could have hoped for. Around one million people saw the president lying in state as his funeral train came back to Springfield. Embalmed by the firm of Brown & Alexander, Lincoln's body was attended throughout its long trip home by the firm's staff, including

the very bearded Henry P. Cattell. They were, according to
the brochure,

> able to keep Lincoln in a presentable viewing condition
> with the help of local embalmers and undertakers along
> the way. Though often noting these discolorations, news-
> paper accounts generally reported favorably on the presi-
> dent's appearance.

Another brochure, this one devoted to the nearby tomb of
Lincoln, concludes with the thought that since thousands of
people come to Springfield every year to visit Lincoln's
tomb, then "the National Lincoln Monument Association
completed its task of erecting a tribute that conveys the
country's estimate placed upon his life, virtues, and public
services."

While I appreciate the local boosterism behind that sentiment, in a museum across town there is another object that
is the best indication of the esteem for Lincoln I have ever
seen—more than the marble tomb, more than even the marble Lincoln Memorial in Washington, D.C., more than any
book, statue, lock of hair, bloodstained collar, top hat, or
plaque.

Any old forgettable rich guy might warrant a marble tomb,
an obelisk, or elaborate sculptures after death, but you know
you are regarded with a ridiculous, religious amount of awe
when they put your dug-up drainpipe in a museum. It's on
display here in Springfield at the Lincoln Home National
Historic Site, a complex including the home the Lincolns
lived in from 1844 until they left for Washington in 1861, as
well as several neighboring houses, each a museum named

for its occupants in 1860. Tim Townsend of the National Park Service, the site's historian, was showing me around one of these museums, the Dean House, when I spotted the drainpipe of devotion.

Townsend directs me to look at a photograph of a political rally held here during the 1860 presidential campaign. Throngs of people are crowded in front of the two-story house. One man towers over them—Abraham Lincoln, in a white suit.

So I'm just one of the countless pilgrims who made their way to this house paying homage to that man.

"Even during the Civil War," Townsend says, "when the Lincolns were in Washington, Civil War soldiers were training at a camp here in Springfield and some of them would write home, 'Drove past the president's house today,' 'Rode past, visited the president's house.' The family that was renting were very accommodating to people knocking and just letting them in. So really the visitation even started as early as that. And after Mr. Lincoln's assassination, that's when the house first became kind of an icon. People wanted to connect with the president, so they came here.

"The oldest Lincoln son, Robert, ultimately ended up with sole ownership of the home. He maintained it as rental property. He complained about it, having to deal with this house. In fact there's a quote in a letter that he'd owned that house until it 'ruined him,' just having to deal with landlord stuff. But he couldn't quite part with the house. Finally, in 1887, he did decide to donate the Lincoln home to the state of Illinois on the condition that it be well maintained and free of access, meaning free of charge. So that makes it one of the earliest publicly held historic sites in the nation. As of 1887 on, it was opened as a historic site."

"And did Robert ever come and stay in it occasionally?" I ask. "You know how sometimes"—I learned this from a cabdriver I had once in Memphis—"Lisa-Marie Presley still stays at Graceland?"

"As far as we know he did not. He did end up visiting in Springfield a time or two. There's one episode where we know he went in and identified the rooms and things like that, but nothing more than that. The National Park Service began operation of the Lincoln home in 1972, when the state of Illinois donated it."

Townsend opens the door to Lincoln's house, taking off his Stetson hat. I have been looking forward to this moment for years. I must have only seen black-and-white photos, however, because I am unprepared for the way it looks. And it looks Christmasy.

"I don't know why I keep thinking about Graceland," I tell Townsend, "but it's so red and green and garish. This isn't how I pictured it."

"Yes," he says. "That does surprise a lot of people. In 1860, it's the start of the Victorian in terms of decorative elements. If you were able to get the latest stuff in 1860 and you were stylish, there was the fairly recent technology to produce these bright colors."

"Is that Lincoln's original couch?" I ask.

"I believe that it is, yes."

I can't quite put my finger on why I'm not really feeling anything. I came here to get closer to Lincoln. So why is it that I feel closer to him sitting on my couch reading my paperback copy of his *Selected Speeches and Writings* than I do here in actual Springfield staring at the actual couch where he read his beloved newspapers and Shakespeare?

Townsend must be reading my mind. He says, "This home really reflects Mrs. Lincoln more than Mr. Lincoln. Mrs. Lincoln came from a very wealthy background down in Lexington, Kentucky, and the home reflects her taste and what she was used to. This is her sphere, this is the stuff she really cared about and was good at, and he was more often downtown working. But this home played a pivotal role during the campaign. Folks came to visit, there were open houses, things like that. Because Lincoln did not go out and campaign—it was considered improper at that time."

Upstairs, he says, "The wallpaper in the bedroom suite area is an exact copy of what Mary had here, and this is the only area in the home where we know exactly what the color and pattern was, and this is a reproduction of that. And there again, that bright blue surprises a lot of people."

"Yeah, it's hideous," I say.

"This is the space Mary would use for some quiet time. She suffered from migraine headaches quite often and this would be a place perhaps she could get away."

After Lincoln died, Mary and her two remaining sons Robert and Tad moved to Chicago. Mary returned to Springfield a couple of times, but she never lived in this house again.

"I think it was just too painful for her," Townsend says. "By that time, before she died, she had seen her husband assassinated and three of her four sons die. And her fourth son—they kind of grew apart."

"That's a nice way of putting it," I agree. He is referring to Mary Todd Lincoln's falling-out with Robert Todd Lincoln.

At the time of her husband's assassination, Mary had already buried two young sons. And so her husband, nothing if not empathetic, indulged her eccentricities, including allowing the séances she hosted in the White House in an effort to contact her dead little boys. Then, not only was her husband murdered, she was sitting next to him when it happened. Six years later, her son Tad died too. It would be insane if a mother and wife had endured that much grief without going mad.

In 1875, concluding that Mary was mentally unstable, Robert had her followed by Pinkerton detectives. He hired the private eyes to protect his mother, but he also assigned them to report back with any suspicious behavior. Such as summoning a waiter to her hotel room and demanding to see "the tallest man in the dining room," for example. So Robert attempted to have his mother committed to an institution. When she refused, he instigated a nasty public insanity trial. His mother was institutionalized not far from Chicago. Though she eventually got herself released, she never forgave her son.

I ask Townsend, "When you're telling the story here to just the regular tourists, do you go into any of that stuff, like the insanity trial, or Robert not being buried here because his wife couldn't stand his mom?"

"It's not really our primary story here," he says. "But people do ask and we'll talk about, at least our opinions. What the staff generally tends to do is say that Mary's mental health is a complicated issue. Should Robert have done what he did or shouldn't he have? Quite often, I guess kind of like a biographer would, you start to become attached to the people you're talking about, and we end up, I think, becoming Mary defenders here, so to speak. Not blatantly, but we do cut the lady some slack."

He continues, "I mentioned how important the home was, and there were a lot of newspaper articles at the time of Lincoln's nomination and election where they're very complimentary—what a pleasant home Abe Lincoln has and complimenting Mary. And she did spend a lot of time polishing his rough edges and getting him sophisticated enough to go to the next level. She was very politically astute, and they enjoyed discussing politics together. They had this partnership almost, politically."

In Lincoln's bedroom, Townsend points out, "The desk in the corner is an original, as well as the shaving mirror. That mirror surprises a lot of people, too. Attorney Lincoln who lived here in Springfield always shaved, and didn't start growing a beard until the time of his election."

The little mirror is hung on the wall at the perfect height to frame Lincoln's face. I have a six-foot-four-inch friend— Lincoln's exact height—who told me that when he came here he could see his face framed perfectly in the mirror. I want to see mine in it too, but I'm Secretary of State Seward's height—five foot four—so I have to jump up a foot to see my face in the mirror, which sets off an alarm.

*

The Lincoln depot is a short walk from the Lincoln home. Except for the forlorn fact that this is where the president-elect would depart for the city of his death, it's an otherwise nice old brick train station. A plaque erected in 1914 by the Springfield Chapter of the Illinois Daughters of the American Revolution lists his Farewell Address of February 11, 1861. "My friends," it begins,

> no one, not in my situation, can appreciate my feeling of sadness at this parting. To this place, and the kindness of these people, I owe every thing. Here I have lived a quarter of a century, and have passed from a young to an old man. Here my children have been born, and one is buried. I now leave, not knowing when, or whether ever, I may return, with a task before me greater than that which rested upon Washington.

That phrase "whether ever, I may return" is pretty poignant considering he would return, but in a long black casket decked with silver stars and fringe.

"I bid you an affectionate farewell," he told his friends and neighbors. Then he waved good-bye.

The hands Lincoln waved good-bye with are there wherever I go, waiting for me. Sculptor Leonard Volk came to Springfield in 1860, two days after Abraham Lincoln received the Republican Party's presidential nomination. At Lincoln's house, Volk made casts of the hands. The reason the right hand is larger than the left is that Lincoln's right hand was swollen from all the congratulatory shaking.

After Lincoln's assassination everyone wanted a piece of him. And I do mean right after. A member of the audience that night at Ford's later recalled, "As [Lincoln] was carried out of the Theatre, the blood from the wound in his head dropped along the floor, and many of the people dipped their handkerchiefs therein to preserve as a sacred souvenir of the beloved President."

When sculptor Augustus Saint-Gaudens learned of Volk's casts of the president's hands, he immediately set out to raise money to purchase them to donate to the Smithsonian, where the originals are on display today. Saint-Gaudens established a subscription service where patrons could purchase plaster or bronze casts of the originals. Ever since, Lincoln's hands have been scattered to the winds. Besides the Smithsonian, I have seen them at least nine times, in Washington, Chicago, Springfield, Quebec, at Robert Todd Lincoln's Vermont house Hildene, and at Daniel Chester French's house in the Berkshires (where French consulted them for his statue for the Lincoln Memorial, though, ultimately, he modeled the hands of the marble colossus after his own).

William Dean Howells once described seeing the hands at a party in a New York home. One partygoer in particular seemed drawn to them. He picked them up, held the hands in his own, and asked the host to whom they belonged. And when he heard that they were the hands of Abraham Lincoln, the man, Edwin Booth, silently placed them back upon the shelf.

*

Until the Lincoln Memorial was dedicated on the Mall in 1922, the main shrine for Lincoln pilgrims in Washington, D.C., was east of the Capitol, the Freedmen's Memorial in Lincoln Park, dedicated on April 14, 1876, the eleventh anniversary of the assassination.

At the dedication, Frederick Douglass gave a speech. About Thomas Ball's problematic sculpture of a standing Abraham Lincoln with a shirtless slave kneeling at his feet, the most specific thing Douglass says is that it is a "highly interesting object." Douglass never says he likes it, probably because he doesn't. Meant to commemorate the signing of the Emancipation Proclamation on January 1, 1863, the intent was to portray the Great Emancipator freeing a slave from his shackles. Nevertheless, it's still a little icky the way the black man looks like he's bowing down to the white man. Frederick Douglass, no dope, would have noticed.

The stories behind the sculpture are more interesting than the thing itself. When Charlotte Scott, a freed slave, heard of Lincoln's assassination, she had the idea that all her fellow freedmen should build a monument in his memory. Scott, the story goes, donated the first five dollars she ever earned. Archer Alexander, the model for the slave, was the last runaway slave to be returned to his master under the Fugitive Slave Act.

"This is no day for malice," Frederick Douglass said to those assembled, including President Grant. He marvels that such a gathering would have been unthinkable before Lincoln's time. The rest of Douglass's speech is remarkable, one of the most unflinching, truthful, well-argued celebrations of Abraham Lincoln I've ever read. In front of Grant and everybody, Douglass calls Lincoln "pre-eminently the white man's president," pointing out that Lincoln's position before the war, and at the beginning of the war, was simply to prevent the extension of slavery. He cared more about saving the Union than he did about freeing the slaves. "We are at best only his stepchildren," Douglass complains. He enumerates Lincoln's slowness to take up the cause of slaves, dwelling on the disappointment, Douglass's frustration welling up inside him and squirting out his mouth. Everything he's just said is true, but so is the next thing:

> Can any colored man, or any white man friendly to the freedom of all men, ever forget the night which followed the first day of January, 1863, when the world was to see if Abraham Lincoln would prove to be as good as his word? I shall never forget that memorable night, when in a distant city I waited and watched at a public meeting, with three thousand others not less anxious than myself, for the word of deliverance which we have heard read today. Nor shall I ever forget the outburst of joy and thanksgiving that rent the air when the lightning brought to us the Emancipation Proclamation. In that happy hour we forgot all delay, and forgot all tardiness.

Douglass was there, a few blocks across Capitol Hill from here, when Lincoln delivered the Second Inaugural Address. And Douglass's speech echoes Lincoln's the way it charts the president's progress through the war, quoting Lincoln in 1864 saying that "if slavery is not wrong, nothing is wrong," then citing that threat in the Second Inaugural that he would continue the war "until each drop of blood drawn by the lash shall have been paid for by one drawn by the sword."

This is all very specific. That is the most impressive thing about it. Douglass is actually trying to remember Lincoln, what he did, what he said, how he changed. The problem with the fog of history, with the way the taboo against speak-

ing ill of the dead tends to edit memorials down to saying
nothing much more than the deceased subject's name, is
that all the specifics get washed away, leaving behind some
universal nobody. Martin Luther King Jr.'s last speech, in
which he correctly prophesied that he "might not get there
with you" to the Promised Land is all that's remembered of
what he said. And that is astonishing. But that speech also
contains clear-cut political suggestions for the very present
moment, including a plea to those assembled to boycott the
Coca-Cola Company "because they haven't been fair in their
hiring policies."

Frederick Douglass, by calling forth Lincoln the man,
by mapping how time and circumstance and experience
changed him and deepened him and emboldened him to not
just say the right thing and not just personally do the right
thing, but make right the law, is the most meaningful of all
possible tributes. Douglass, a former slave, marvels that the
"infinite wisdom has seldom sent any man into the world
better fitted for his mission than Abraham Lincoln."

I brought Douglass's speech with me to the Freedmen's
Memorial and I reread it, occasionally glancing up at the
statue. As I'm scrutinizing the plaque about Charlotte Scott,
a black woman with white hair walks past, staring at me.
Smiling, she yells, "Emancipation Proclamation!" She turns
away with a wave, calling out over her shoulder, "Freed the
slaves, amen!"

President James A. Garfield in Long Branch, New Jersey (based on an engraving on the cover of Harper's Weekly, *September 24, 1881). Seven presidents, Garfield included, vacationed in Long Branch, the Hamptons of the Gilded Age. Shot on July 2 in a Washington train station, Garfield was expected to survive. However, summertime in the nation's capital—a former swamp —saps even the healthiest citizens' will to live. Thus Garfield and his doctors believed the sea air at the Jersey shore would restore the president's health. They were wrong. Garfield died there on September 19, 1881.*

CHAPTER TWO

The most famous thing ever said about President James A. Garfield is about how nobody has any idea who the hell he was. A citizen doing even the most halfhearted research about the man comes across, again and again, mention of Thomas Wolfe's 1934 story "The Four Lost Men":

> Garfield, Arthur, Harrison, and Hayes, time of my father's time, blood of his blood, life of his life, . . . were the lost Americans: their gravely vacant and bewhiskered faces mixed, melted, swam together in the sea depths of a past intangible, immeasurable, and unknowable as the buried city of Persepolis. And they were lost. For who was Garfield, martyred man, and who had seen him in the streets of life? Who could believe that his footfalls ever sounded on a lonely pavement? Who had heard the casual and familiar tones of Chester Arthur? Where was Harrison? Where was Hayes? Which had the whiskers, which the burnsides: Which was which? Were they not lost?

To Wolfe, as to most of us, James A. Garfield is the deadest of dead men, so faceless that even a third grader who just got a gold star on her Garfield report would be hard-pressed to pick him out of a lineup. Wolfe doubts if his four lost men took corporeal form at all, wondering if they ever had "trembling lips, numb entrails, pounding hearts."

In the sweaty summer of 1881, to the American people,

that's all Garfield was—a body. In the two and a half months separating his July 2 shooting and his death on September 19, the people were obsessed, transfixed, following the daily, sometimes hourly, dispatches on the dying president's condition as if the progression of his blood poisoning was the fourth quarter of the NBA Finals, as if a movie star in a tuxedo were slowly opening the Best Picture envelope at the Academy Awards. The citizenry not only scoured their newspapers for word of every rise and fall of Garfield's temperature, his blood pressure, pulse, swelling, each "free discharge of healthy-looking pus." People regularly stopped by newspapers offices so as to check on the latest telegraphed update from the president's surgeons. On July 29, for example, a wire issued at 8:30 A.M. notes that Garfield "has had quite a nap since the noon bulletin was issued." On August 8, the surgeons reported that it had "become necessary to make another opening to facilitate the escape of pus." On August 11, at 12:30 P.M., "his skin is moist, but without undue perspiration."

To our forebears, Garfield had eyes that opened and closed, sweat glands and pus, the pus getting an awful lot of play. He had skin and it was moist. Americans knew more details about Garfield's breath and blood than they did about their own lungs, their personal hearts. How intimate. How embarrassing.

An excerpt from the diary of the president's daughter, Mollie, is displayed in the museum at the James A. Garfield National Historic Site in Mentor, Ohio. On September 29, 1881, ten days after her father's death, Mollie wrote, "It is something really beautiful to see how much the people had gotten to love Papa through all his sickness."

Hanging underneath Mollie's words is Garfield's death mask, a shock. Cast in bronze by the sculptor Augustus Saint-Gaudens, the dead man's face bears little resemblance to the photographs of the healthy roundness of Garfield's prime. The mask is gaunt and long. Garfield wasted away after the shooting. He lost eighty pounds. Thanks to the death mask, the visitor can see what Garfield's family saw— a big man shrunk small.

Witnessing the physical evidence of what Garfield went through, what his wife and children endured day after day, the fact that this man shriveled to the grave all because American voters picked him to be president, well, it seems tacky that we forgot him.

Thankfully, the story of Garfield's death is more interesting than the story of his life. His pre-presidential bio can be crammed into the following respectable sentence: The last president born in a log cabin, Garfield grew up with his widowed mother in Ohio, eked his way through college, became a college professor who moonlighted as a preacher, married his wife, Lucretia, in 1858, fathered five children, was a Union general in the Civil War, and served the people of Ohio in the House of Representatives from 1863 to 1880.

But back to his death. It is the story of this self-made man's collision course with two of the most self-serving, self-centered, self-absorbed egomaniacs of the late nineteenth century—Garfield's nemesis, Senator Roscoe Conkling, and the assassin, Charles Guiteau. The Garfield assassination is an opera of arrogance, a spectacle of greed, a galling, appalling epic of egomania dramatizing the lust for pure power, shameless and raw. And where else can a story like that start but in New York?

On Wall Street stands the building that got Garfield killed. A solid gray edifice festooned with columns, it has been recently abandoned. A few months ago, it was the Regent Wall Street, a luxury hotel that opened its doors to relief workers when the nearby World Trade Center fell down, a luxury hotel that hosted the reception for Liza Minnelli's wedding, a wedding in which the "co-best men" were Michael Jackson and his brother, Tito. But like the marriage, the hotel went belly-up. The doors are locked. Paper is taped over the windows.

This district, unwittingly responsible for Garfield's end, is where Herman Melville's *Moby-Dick* begins. Ishmael, taking a walk downtown before shipping out, says of the island of Manhattan, "Commerce surrounds it with her surf." And throughout the nineteenth century, all of the U.S. government's plunder from said commerce, the taxes and tariffs squeezed out of all the ships at port, would be tallied up (and more often than not, pocketed by the customs employees) here, at the New York Custom House.

While we're on the subject of Melville, it's worth pointing out that he worked in this building as a deputy customs inspector between 1866 and 1885. Nineteen years, and he never got a raise—four dollars a day, six days a week. He was by then a washed-up writer, forgotten and poor. I used to find this subject heartbreaking, a waste: the greatest living American author was forced to spend his days writing tariff reports instead of novels. But now, knowing what I know about the sleaze of the New York Custom House, and the honorable if bitter decency with which Melville did his job, I have come to regard literature's loss as the republic's gain. Great writers are a dime a dozen in New York. But an honest customs inspector in the Gilded Age? Unheard of.

Before the institution of an income tax in 1913, the New York Custom House collected an astounding two-thirds of the federal government's revenue. The New York customs collector was allowed, even encouraged, to wet his beak in the oceans of cash. Thus was the position the most lucrative job in American government, a post with bottomless potential for embezzlement and fraud. For example, an 1865 commission investigating the rampant graft by the employees of the New York Custom House estimated that the government might be losing as much as $25 million a year.

The customs collector was a political appointee. And despite the position's bearing on the federal coffers, in the 1870s the New York State Republican Party machine controlled the job. Senator Roscoe Conkling, a flamboyant, grandiose hothead, ruled the party. Chester Alan Arthur, Conkling's best friend, ran the Custom House. In 1878, in a bold power grab, President Rutherford B. Hayes stood up to his fellow Republican, the all-powerful Conkling, fired "Chet" Arthur in the name of civil service reform, and waited to install a replacement until Conkling and his fellow senators were in recess.

Momentary Hayes detour: Hayes was no stranger to power plays. In 1876, Hayes wasn't so much elected president as installed in the presidency thanks to a congressional electoral commission. It came to be called the Compromise of 1877. What happened was Democrat Samuel Tilden received more popular votes than Hayes, though four states were too close to call. In January 1877, the electoral commission, comprised of an equal number of Democrats and Republicans, was at an impasse. The Republicans persuaded the Democrats to "elect" Hayes by agreeing to end Reconstruction. (Hard to believe that the candidate who lost the popular vote could actually become the president of the United States. Luckily, that kind of travesty never happened again.) In the compromise, the Republicans promised to withdraw federal troops from the South. Why was the U.S. Army still occupying the South twelve years after the Civil War? To safeguard the civil rights of black citizens. By pulling the troops out of Dixie, the Republicans were selling out the freed slaves. Which makes the Compromise of 1877 one of the tourist attractions on the road to watching the party of Lincoln morph into the Republican Party we all know and love today.

Returning to President Hayes versus Senator Conkling with regards to the New York Custom House: Conkling would retaliate against Hayes for firing Chester Arthur by delivering a spiteful speech at the next New York Republican convention, pooh-poohing self-proclaimed reformers like Hayes as hypocrites whose sole purpose was to "lament the sins of other people." Thanks to Conkling, President Hayes would be out of a job come 1880, when his own party would dump him.

Nowadays, the national nominating conventions are foregone conclusions in which the party zealots spend a few days and a few million dollars applauding themselves while balloons bounce off their shellacked hairdos on TV. But the 1880 Republican National Convention in summertime Chicago was unpredictable, a hissy fit on the verge of riot.

Two factions within the Republican Party were engaged in a civil war about the Civil War. Their bickering can be boiled down to how each faction felt about one man, former president Ulysses S. Grant. Grant's backers, led by Senator Conkling, called themselves the Stalwarts. The Stalwarts ar-

rived in Chicago bent on nominating Grant for an unprecedented third term. They favored equating the rise of southern Democrats with the threat of igniting the War Between
the States all over again, a tactic known as "waving the
bloody shirt," the shirt being a blue Union uniform stained
red with its dead wearer's blood. For example, here is one
whopper of a bloody-shirt speech the ex–Union colonel
Robert Ingersoll once delivered for the Hayes campaign:

> Every man that shot Union soldiers was a Democrat.
> Every man that denied Union prisoners even the worm-
> eaten crust of famine, and when some poor, emaciated
> Union patriot, driven to insanity by famine, saw in an in-
> sane dream the face of his mother, and she beckoned him
> and he followed, hoping to press her lips once again
> against his fevered face, and when he stepped one step
> beyond the dead line the wretch that put the bullet
> through his loving, throbbing heart was and is a Demo-
> crat. Every man that loved slavery better than liberty was
> a Democrat. The man that assassinated Abraham Lincoln
> was a Democrat. . . . Every man that wanted the privilege
> of whipping another man to make him work for him for
> nothing and pay him with lashes on his naked back, was a
> Democrat. Every man that raised bloodhounds to pursue
> human beings was a Democrat. Every man that clutched
> from shrieking, shuddering, crouching mothers, babes
> from their breasts, and sold them into slavery, was a
> Democrat. . . . Soldiers, every scar you have on your
> heroic bodies was given you by a Democrat. Every scar,
> every arm that is lacking, every limb that is gone, is a sou-
> venir of a Democrat. I want you to recollect it.

So who, argued the bloody-shirt, Stalwart Grant fans in 1880, could better stand down the Democrats and lead the country than the hero of Appomattox, the man who won the war and thus the peace?

Problem was, Grant had already served two clunky terms preceding Hayes. Republicans calling themselves the Half-Breeds, led by Maine senator James G. Blaine, were dead set against the return of Grant, seeing the old general's administrative corruption and abandonment of civil service reform as an embarrassment. Conkling and Blaine had been sworn enemies for years, ever since Blaine had made fun of Conkling's "turkey gobbler strut" on the Senate floor. Thus was the convention deadlocked.

With a century and change between the 1880 convention and now, I'll admit I rolled my eyes at the ideological hair-splitting, wondering how a group of people who more or less agreed with one another about most issues could summon forth such stark animosity. Thankfully, we Americans have evolved, our hearts made larger, our minds more open, welcoming the negligible differences among our fellows with compassion and respect. As a Democrat who voted for Al Gore in the 2000 presidential election, an election suspiciously tipped to tragic Republican victory because of a handful of contested ballots in the state of Florida, I, for one, would never dream of complaining about the votes siphoned in that state by my fellow liberal Ralph Nader, who convinced citizens whose hopes for the country differ little from my own to vote for him, even though had those votes gone to Gore, perhaps those citizens might have spent their free time in the years to come more pleasurably pursuing leisure activities, such as researching the sacrifice of Family

Garfield, instead of attending rallies and protests against wars they find objectionable, not to mention the money saved on aspirin alone considering they'll have to pop a couple every time they read the newspaper, wondering if the tap water with which they wash down the pills is safe enough to drink considering the corporate polluter lobbyists now employed at the EPA.

But meanwhile, back at the 1880 Republican convention in Chicago, enter James Abram Garfield of Ohio. He was attractive as a candidate for the precise reason he's a nondescript president—his bland composure. Congressman Garfield had come to Chicago in support of a third, hopeless candidate, Treasury Secretary John Sherman, brother of the Georgia-torching General William T. Taking the podium just after Conkling had almost incited a riot while giving a speech for Grant, Garfield said:

> This assemblage seems to be a human ocean in tempest. I have seen the sea lashed into fury and tossed into spray, and its grandeur moves the soul of the dullest man; but I remember that it is not the billows, but the calm level of the sea, from which all heights and depths are measured.

After reminding the Republican Party of its past, collaborative glories—*we* ended slavery, *we* saved the Union—Garfield encouraged his fellow Republicans to look past the present hubbub and think about their common goal, the election, an election that, months away, would be won or lost "in the quiet melancholy days of November."

While Conkling complained that Garfield's emotional

oceanography had made him "sea-sick," most of the other delegates considered Garfield dry land. They were relieved to agree on something, someone.

So, the Half-Breeds and Stalwarts compromised on Garfield. For the rest of his soon-to-end life, Garfield would be trapped in the middle of the two factions, an Archie forever whiplashed between the Veronica of Conkling and the Betty of Blaine. Blaine's Half-Breeds cringed at Garfield's letter accepting the nomination because, referring to political appointments, Garfield pledged to "seek and receive the information and assistance of those whose knowledge of the communities in which the duties are to be performed best qualifies them to aid in making the wisest choice." The Blainiacs, as they were called, saw this as an endorsement of the spoils system and thus a score for Conkling, the boss of New York. A fear they already harbored given Garfield's vice-presidential choice—Conkling's friend, former New York customs collector Chester Alan Arthur, the most infamous spoilsman of all, a man who celebrated his lofty new place in American history by doing what he did best—shopping.

Nominee Garfield went back to his Ohio farm in Mentor. The National Park Service has since restored his gray clapboard home, including the front porch he used in his front porch campaign. At the time, on-the-road glad-handing and stump speeches were considered beneath a presidential candidate's dignity, and so the voters came to Garfield. They loitered in his yard, waiting for the candidate to come in from his fields to say a few words. Such as, "Ladies and gentlemen, all the doors of my house are open to you. The hand of every member of my family is outstretched to you. Our hearts greet you, and we ask you to come in." Notice he doesn't ask them to sit down—Mrs. Garfield fed visitors standing up so they wouldn't linger.

Allison Sharaba, the Garfield home's operations manager, shows me around, pointing at quaint Victorian rooms and spidery blue wallpaper. In the library, I spot eleven volumes of *The Works of Charles Sumner*. Sumner, the Massachusetts senator, was famously beaten up on the Senate floor in 1856 by a pro-slavery South Carolinian driven mad by Sumner's abolitionist rhetoric. Not that Sumner's fellow Republicans didn't also ponder punching him over the years. Sumner was everything Garfield was not—a brilliant, bitchy, righteous and self-righteous blabbermouth, the pepper jack to Garfield's cream cheese. As Sumner lay dying in 1874, Garfield wrote in his diary that "Sumner was the most scholarly man in public life," remarking, "Sumner was my friend; though I have never been blind to his follies yet I have believed in him as an honest and faithful man."

Garfield and Sumner were known as the most voracious readers on Capitol Hill, frequently bumping into each other in the stacks of the Library of Congress while their fellow legislators were probably side by side at bordellos and bars. The sad thing about Garfield's eleven volumes of Sumner's *Works* is that it's a fifteen-volume set; the final book in the series wasn't published until two years after Garfield's death. Garfield's assassination meant he would miss out on so much, from the double wedding of his children held in this very library, to finishing out his first presidential term. But I would imagine he would also have mourned all the books he never got to read. *Huckleberry Finn*, for starters, wasn't published until 1884.

Garfield's diaries are low-key; I doubt even he would have

read them, and he read everything. What passes for dramatic conflict is witnessing him, during his tenure in the House, fidget through congressional committee meetings when the only place he wants to be is holed up with his new twenty-six-volume shipment of the complete works of Goethe. He tries to cheer himself up about the political and personal hassles keeping him from German poetry, writing, "Perhaps that study of literature is fullest which we steal from daily duties."

If there is a recurring theme in Garfield's diaries it's this: *I'd rather be reading*. That might sound dull and perfunctory, but Garfield's book fever was a sickness. Take, for example, the commencement address he delivered at his alma mater Hiram College in the summer of 1880. Traditionally, these pep talks to college graduates are supposed to shove young people into the future with a briefcase bulging with infinitive verbs: to make, to produce, to do. Mr. Loner McBookworm, on the other hand, stands up and breaks it to his audience, the future achievers of America, that the price of the supposedly fulfilling attainment of one's personal and professional dream is the irritating way it cuts into one's free time. He tells them,

> It has occurred to me that the thing you have, that all men have enough of, is perhaps the thing that you care for the least, and that is your leisure—the leisure you have to think; the leisure you have to be let alone; the leisure you have to throw the plummet into your mind, and sound the depth and dive for things below.

The only thing stopping this address from turning into a slacker parable is the absence of the word "dude." Keep in mind that at that moment Garfield was a presidential candidate. The guy who theoretically wants the country's most demanding, hectic, brain-dive-denying job stands before these potential gross national product producers advising them to treat leisure "as your gold, as your wealth, as your treasure." As Garfield left the podium, every scared kid in the room could probably hear the sound of the stock market crashing him back to his old room at his parents' house where he'd have plenty of free time to contemplate hanging himself with his boyhood bedsheets.

As for me, coming across that downbeat commencement speech was the first time I really liked Garfield. It's hard to have strong feelings about him. Before, I didn't mind him, and of course I sympathized with his bum luck of a death. But I find his book addiction endearing, even a little titillating considering that he would sneak away from the house and the House to carry on a love affair with Jane Austen. In his diary he raves about an afternoon spent rearranging his library in a way that reminds me of the druggy glow you can hear in Lou Reed's voice on "Heroin."

Upstairs at the house in Mentor, Allison shows me Garfield's private office. She says, "This is where he liked to retreat, maybe at the end of the day, when he needed to get away from the campaign life and children and everything. He would come in here and read."

She points at a lopsided armchair, says Garfield had it "specially made for him. He would lean his back up against the high side of the chair and flip his legs over the low side." It's an appealing image, our respectable presidential paragon slouched in a posture with all the decorum of a teenager plopped on top a beanbag.

"That's John Brown, isn't it?" I ask, about a portrait hanging on the wall.

"Yes," she answers, "that's John Brown. The story behind it is just strange." She says that during the museum's renovation, in order to restore the office to its Garfield-era appearance, period photographs of the room were consulted. "Apparently," she continues, "there was a portrait about the same size and shape and we didn't really know who it was, so the decision was made to put that up there. John Brown was, I think, too much of a radical for James Garfield to actually have his portrait in his office, but I don't know if there's another reason other than they just needed to fill the space."

According to his diaries, Garfield had a friend in Mentor and when he stopped by the man's house they would make a point of singing "John Brown's Body" together, a song that Garfield's assassin also enjoyed. During his murder trial, one of Charles Guiteau's many bizarre outbursts was singing "John Brown's Body" to the court, claiming that if he was executed for killing the president, his soul would also, like John Brown's in the song, march on.

Charles J. Guiteau is James A. Garfield's cracked mirror image. Both men were raised in the Midwest (Garfield in Ohio, Guiteau in Illinois) by a single, widowed parent (Garfield's father died when he was not quite two and Guiteau lost his mother). Both men were devout Christians who dabbled in preaching. Both men were born poor but longed for education and a better life. Both were ardent Republicans. And yet Garfield—dependable, industrious, and loved—was everything Guiteau was not.

Guiteau's father, Luther Guiteau, was as bizarre and remote as Garfield's mom was encouraging and ever-present.

And so, after dropping out of the University of Michigan after one lonesome, miserable year, Guiteau, most likely to impress his hard-to-impress dad, moved in with the religious cult his father admired.

*

One winter night in my kitchen, as I poured peppermint tea into my friend Lisa's cup, she said that she liked my teapot. I told her that my happy yellow teapot has a kinky backstory involving a nineteenth-century vegetarian sex cult in upstate New York whose members lived for three decades as self-proclaimed "Bible communists" before incorporating into the biggest supplier of dinnerware to the American food-service industry, not to mention harboring their most infamous resident, an irritating young maniac who, years after he moved away, was hanged for assassinating President Garfield.

It goes without saying that in order for me to buy my teapot on the cheap at the Oneida, Ltd., outlet store at the Sherrill Shopping Plaza, the second coming of Jesus Christ had to have taken place in the year 70 A.D. To the Oneida Community, 70 A.D., the year the temple in Jerusalem was destroyed, marks the beginning of the New Jerusalem. Which means we've all been living in heaven on earth for nearly two thousand years. Everyone knows there is no marriage in heaven (though one suspects there's no shortage of it in hell). So, the Oneidans said, we're here in heaven, already saved and perfect in the eyes of God, so let's move upstate and sleep around. (I'm paraphrasing.)

John Humphrey Noyes, the founder, leader, and guru of the utopian Oneida Community, wrote in 1837, "In a holy community, there is no more reason why sexual intercourse should be restricted by law, than why eating and drinking should be—and there is as little occasion for shame in the one case as in the other."

Any theologian who assured his fellow Victorians that fondling one's neighbor's wife is as ordinary as frying an egg was bound to attract a following. In 1848, Noyes and forty-five cohorts moved to Oneida to pursue what they called "group marriage," eventually building the three-story brick mansion house that remains today as a combination museum, apartment building, and hotel. My sister Amy, three-year-old nephew Owen, and I spent a night there.

Owen recognized the mansard-roofed mansion straightaway—not as an old religious commune, but as a building he'd seen on *Scooby-Doo*. "Haunted house," he whispered as Amy yanked him from his car seat, oohing like a cartoon ghost all the way through check-in. After dinner at a nearby steakhouse, in which my sister pleads, "Owen, please, *please* don't use your hair as a napkin," Amy eventually returns to our room to wash the ketchup off her sticky son while I sneak around the dark and quiet halls, vainly hoping to bump into fornicating specters, or, if this really were *Scooby-Doo*, high school kids dressed up like spooks to scare away nosy interlopers like me. I sit at a desk in the comfortable library, perusing the complete works of Dickens and an old book about China by an American advertising man entitled *Four Hundred Million Customers*. "It probably never occurred to you," he wrote, "that banditry around the head waters of the Yangtsze would affect the quality of an English toothbrush." He's right.

The next morning, Joe Valesky, a retired Oneida native

who taught high school American history for thirty-six years, gives me a guided tour. Someday, I hope to be just like him. There are people who look forward to spending their sunset years in the sunshine; it is my own retirement dream to await my death indoors, dragging strangers up dusty staircases while coughing up one of the most thrilling phrases in the English language: "It was on this spot . . ." My fantasy is to one day become a docent.

Valesky points to a yellowing photograph of John Humphrey Noyes hanging on the wall. On paper, Noyes resembles a bearded old-fashioned everyman, your great-grandfather or mine. Seems unthinkable that the head poking out of that starched collar was coming up with dogma about ejaculation. The same thing could be said about this house we traipse around: it looks like the past, which is to say upstanding and chaste, even though its small, clean chambers witnessed more nooky than all the bedrooms on *MTV Cribs* combined.

A corridor of polished woodwork opens onto a courtyard that boasts, I'm told, "the oldest tulip tree in the state of New York." Back inside, I'm shown an antique cabinet in which members of the community, famous for their homegrown produce, dried herbs.

The Oneida Community was an upstate tourist attraction right from the start, second, Valesky says, to Niagara Falls. I'm taking the same guided tour offered a hundred and fifty years ago to prim rubbernecks who came here to peep at sex fiends. I wonder how many of my vacationing forebears went home disappointed? They thought they were taking the train to Gomorrah but instead they got to watch herbs dry. Valesky opens a drawer in the herb cabinet so I can get a whiff. He mentions that back in the day, when one tourist was shown the cabinet she rudely asked her community-member guide, "What's that odor?" To which the guide replied, "Perhaps it's the odor of crushed selfishness." Valesky grins. "How about that for a utopian answer?" To my not particularly utopian nose, crushed selfishness smells a lot like cilantro.

Then Valesky spells out an idea about this region—nick-named the "Burned-over District"—that he had read in a book. I'm pretty sure I've read the same book. But one of the advantages of visiting historic sites as opposed to merely reading about them is the endearing glow of hometown pride. Valesky is a volunteer. Who knows how many times he's said the thing he's about to say? Yet he's clearly in awe of the people who lived here and what they tried to accomplish. He doesn't shy away from their faults—we do spend a few awkward minutes discussing the creepy, sleeping-with-your-teenage-niece aspects of Oneida life. But Valesky's cheerleading for the community is touching. It's also educational. There's a lot to be learned from empathy.

The Burned-over District: In the first half of the nineteenth century, upstate New York erupted with eccentric, quasi-Christian joiners like the Mormons and the Shakers. "These people," Valesky says, "were looking for something between the urban situation, with all its problems, and the frontier, which was beyond the pale in terms of any hope for success. So that's what makes this whole area—the New England area and especially the upstate area—a prime target for the growth of utopian cultures. It was settled, it was civilized, it had local governments. But there was enough open land, there was enough opportunity, so that a new idea could be established and, in the case of Oneida, could flourish."

The distribution of people and dogma, Valesky asserts, was helped by the Erie Canal, followed by the railroad. "I can't help thinking," he admits, "that the railroad, and particularly the spread of the railroad, is something that we can relate to in terms of computers, the World Wide Web. I think it was that fast and that cheap to run a single railroad spur from the main line out to a little community here, out to a little factory there, and that following the canal is what made this area so interesting and which allowed ideas as well as people carrying ideas to spread so quickly that you get terms like 'Burned-over District.' "

I bet Valesky was a good high school history teacher. He might have made a decent movie director too. Every time he looks out the window, he sees farther than I, as if he's about to bark instructions to a cinematographer on a crane, filming a time-lapse epic in which antlike canal diggers dissolve into workmen laying railroad tracks spliced into shots of lit matches and smoking fields giving way to praying Shakers, until Joseph Smith loads up the wagons for the Mormons' first move west and the Oneida Community finally decides to make teapots instead of love.

Paintings of John Humphrey Noyes and his wife Harriet hang at the top of the stairs. Yes, Noyes was married. He was an abolitionist known to compare wifery up north to slavery down south, yet Noyes married Harriet in 1838. He sent her a proposal letter that made up in candor what it lacked in woo. Referring to Harriet not as his sweetheart but as his "yoke-fellow," as if they were to be oxen strapped together hauling hay, Noyes informed her that his intentions toward said yoke-fellow "will be not to monopolize and enslave her heart or my own, but to enlarge and establish both, in the free fellowship of God's universal family." In other words, Harriet, don't wait up.

Noyes married Harriet in their native Vermont, a full decade before leading his flock to Oneida. While his proposal isn't one of history's great love letters—I've received more sentimental invoices from my attorney—Noyes's sympathy for Harriet's childbearing heartbreaks early on in their marriage had a profound influence on the future sexual practices at Oneida, specifically what he came to call "male continence," a sexual technique that's about as fun as it sounds.

Harriet gave birth five times in six years but only one of those children lived. "This experience was what directed my studies and kept me studying," Noyes later recalled. "After our last disappointment I pledged my word to my wife that I would never again expose her to such fruitless suffering." At first, Noyes recounts, he simply vowed not to touch her. Then it occurred to him that genitalia have two functions— the reproductive (which led to the aforementioned catastrophes) and the social. He concluded that one function has little to do with the other and that he could eliminate the possibility of eggs being fertilized by not ejaculating. "I experimented on this idea," he wrote, "and found that the self-control which it requires is not difficult; that my enjoyment was increased; that my wife's experience was very satisfactory, as it had never been before; that we had escaped the horrors and the fear of involuntary propagation."

Noyes broke down the sex act into three parts—the beginning, marked by "the simple *presence* of the male organ in the female," the middle, involving "a series of reciprocal *motions*," and of course the end, an "ejaculatory *crisis* which expels the seed." Naturally, one's thoughts turn to canoeing. Noyes described sex as a day trip to the nearby Niagara River. "The skilled boatman," he asserts, will learn "the wisdom of confining his excursions to the region of easy rowing." If not, it's over the falls, and *splat*.

At the Oneida Community, not ejaculating wasn't just a hobby. It was a whole way of life. In fact, Noyes points out, "The Oneida Community in an important sense owed its existence to the discovery of Male Continence." At its core, the community was about sharing—sharing love, sex, food, chores, money, decisions, time. The only thing the Oneida men were supposed to keep to themselves was their sperm. When I ask Valesky why masturbation was also frowned upon, he replies, "Self-pleasuring takes you away from the group."

One of the corollaries of Noyes's theory of group marriage was a taboo against "special love" and a system of defenses to guard against all kinds of intense passion. Consider the following set of problems and the ingenious way in which they were solved. Young people were always getting crushes. Young people only want to sleep with one another. Older people would like to enjoy sex but they aren't as attractive as younger people. Oneida men are supposed to practice male continence, but perfecting male continence takes practice, and until teenage boys learn how to control themselves, their female partners are in danger of impregnation. So here's what they did. Post-menopausal women deflowered young boys. That way, conception is avoided and older women enjoy the pleasures of the flesh. Young girls, annoyingly prone to falling in love, were ushered into womanhood by an older male, usually by an .experienced boater like

Noyes himself. And, if his proposal to Harriet is any indication, Noyes had a knack for deflecting mushy sentiment by
making a girl feel like part of a team.

The admonition against special love meant not only a ban
on falling in love. It applied to all expressions of over-the-top
passion. For example, a little girl who had grown too fond of
her favorite doll was marched into the kitchen and told to
toss it into the fire. A gifted violin player in danger of becoming a virtuoso and thus too attached to his instrument
handed it over to the Oneida authorities and never played
again. When a visiting Canadian teacher complained that
the community did not foster "genius or special talent,"
Noyes was delighted, replying, "We never expected or desired to produce a Byron, a Napoleon, or a Michelangelo."
You know you've reached a new plateau of group mediocrity
when even a Canadian is alarmed by your lack of individ-
uality.

Where did the other violinists—the ones who were kind
of good but not *too* good—perform? Valesky ushers me into
the grand room he says came to be known as the family hall,
"a re-created nineteenth-century opera house. This," he
says, "is the only room that could hold the entire population
and more, because almost three hundred people were living
here. But beyond that, this was a very public room, so the
public was invited to come to various performances given by
community members. They had an orchestra, they had a
choir, they did little operas, operettas, band concerts, chamber music."

Every night, Valesky says, the group assembled here for a
family meeting in which Noyes led them in discussions of
spiritual and business issues. Valesky points at a pleasant old

photograph of the room, in which people are sitting in rocking chairs or knitting or both. But before enjoying the evening's aggressively second-rate entertainment, they would engage in what they thought of as a cleansing ritual, the enchantingly named Mutual Criticism.

Mutual Criticism required a member of the group to stand up in front of everybody and listen to the enumeration of his or her faults. The bright side of being that night's subject for criticism was the rare treat at Oneida of being the center of attention. The downside was that everyone you knew and loved was allowed, even encouraged, to look into your eyes and ask, "You know what your problem is?"

Reading the accounts of community members' moments in the critical sun, one thing that stands out is how specific the criticisms were. A young man was told that he didn't read enough and that when he did he only "skims things." A guy's guy was picked on for his masculinity because "there is not woman enough about him." Though my personal favorite is the New Englander who was taken to task for his "too frequent mention of Vermont."

Despite its harshness, Mutual Criticism cleared the air, disinfecting the tension that necessarily breeds when human beings live in such close proximity. Perhaps everyone's family unit or roommates should engage in the practice from time to time. I am imagining how my sister might have relished a ritualistic opportunity to discuss my flaws and how they affected her, such as my childhood tic of involuntarily humming aloud that went on throughout the Carter administration which in itself is bad enough until one recalls that my humming coincided with the heyday of "You Light Up My Life."

While a nuclear family is capable of low-key but toxic resentment, a commune is Three Mile Island waiting to happen. In *Sleeping Where I Fall*, his memoir of living on an anarchist collective farm in California in the 1960s, Peter Coyote admits to the way his annoyance with his fellow communards sometimes trumped his laissez-faire ideals, leading him to tape up a list of house rules including, "It's fine if you want to take speed, just don't talk to *me*!"

Regarding Mutual Criticism, Valesky proclaims, "It would relate to personality issues, the whole idea being maintaining group stability, group harmony. Resolving conflicts would all be done by the group such that at the end, there would be a feeling that something has been discussed that needed to be."

Standing in the room where the Mutual Criticism took place, Valesky and I conjecture about how the process went for future assassin Charles Guiteau. (In the glossary of a children's book about the Garfield assassination, one of the vocabulary words kids are supposed to learn by studying Guiteau is "nuisance.")

"Well," Valesky replies, "he was here from 1860 to 1865. Then he left and came back. From what I've read, he was pretty annoying. He was not happy. And yet he stayed here for five years. And they let him come back and then he tries to sue them."

Considering that Oneida's group marriage policy theoretically promised constant sexual trysts, unfortunately for Guiteau those trysts had to be consensual. That no one wanted to sleep with Charles Guiteau is hinted at in his Oneida nickname, "Charles Gitout." After he moved away, moved back, then moved away again to New York City, Guiteau launched a vicious lawsuit against the community, alleging that Noyes's practice of initiating the adolescent girls into womanhood was stunting their growth, producing a generation of sexual dwarves.

Guiteau's Noyes-worshiping father was embarrassed enough about the lawsuit to write letters to New York newspapers denouncing his son and praising the Oneida Community. Noyes, whose own son was living in a mental institution at the time, wrote to Luther Guiteau, "I have no ill will toward [Charles]. I regard him as insane, and I prayed for him last night as sincerely as I ever prayed for my own son, that is now in a Lunatic Asylum." Soon thereafter, Luther Guiteau would reach the same conclusion, that Charles should be committed but for the lack of money to pay for it. This is important. Besides sparing the Oneida Community some grief, if Guiteau had received proper treatment from mental health professionals in a caring, padded facility with locks on the doors, it might have spared James Garfield's life.

Here's a distraction. When researching Luther Guiteau's take on his son's stay at Oneida, I couldn't help but notice that in his letters he refers to the Oneida Community as "the O.C." Coincidentally, *The O.C.* is the name of a nighttime soap opera on television's Fox network I am currently obsessed with. Set in Orange County, California, the show's three biggest stars are Peter Gallagher and Peter Gallagher's legendary pair of eyebrows, eyebrows cozy enough to move into—a home, a couple of rocking chairs with a nose between them like a table piled high with every book you ever loved. And thus, when I see the Oneida Community being referred to as "the O.C.," I cannot help but picture all the ladies of Oneida standing in line to curl up in Peter Gal lagher's eyebrows, trying in vain *not* to feel a special love. (The subject of Peter Gallagher's eyebrows, I realize, is a digression away from the Oneida Community, and yet, I do feel compelled, indeed almost conspiracy theoretically bound to mention that one of the reasons the Oneida Community broke up and turned itself into a corporate teapot factory is that a faction within the group, led by a lawyer named James William Towner, was miffed that the community's most esteemed elders were bogarting the teenage virgins and left in a huff for none other than Orange County, California, where Towner helped organize the Orange County government, became a judge, and picked the spot where the Santa Ana courthouse would be built, a courthouse where, it is reasonable to assume, Peter Gallagher's attorney character on *The O.C.* might defend his clients.)

At Oneida, Charles Guiteau's turns at Mutual Criticism scrutiny repeatedly elicited accusations of "egotism and conceit." This is easy to believe considering that Guiteau's delusions of grandeur would later inspire him to write a book with the immodest title *The Truth,* to say nothing of his belief that President Garfield would appoint him as ambassador to France even though at the time he was a dotty unemployed zero.

One learns more about the Oneida Community by considering Charles Guiteau than the other way around. There are Oneida traits in Guiteau for sure. He always credited the community with inspiring his abstinence from liquor and profanity. He plagiarized Noyes in some of his loony later speeches, especially the bits about the second coming of Christ in 70 A.D. But really, the fact that the commune put up with such an exasperating egomaniac for five full years speaks volumes about the Oneida Community's capacity for tolerance. Pondering this, Valesky says, "That's an interesting part of my understanding of what went on here. If that kind of an individual could be accepted and maintain a relationship here as long as he did, it's remarkable."

One impulse Guiteau shared with his Oneida fellows was a yearning to be part of a group, to commune. Even his most deliriously selfish act—overturning the will of the electorate by shooting the president—was conceived and executed as a tribute to the Stalwart faction within the Republican Party. After he did it he proclaimed, "I am a stalwart of the Stalwarts."

As we stand in Oneida's family hall, Joe Valesky tells me that when he first volunteered as a guide here, he spent a lot of time thinking about the men and women who came here to lead such eccentric lives. "What was it like when these people were born in that generation of Americans?" he wondered, continuing, "So at that point I came across Jonathan Edwards and his sermon 'Sinners in the Hands of an Angry God.' Do you know it?"

Do I ever. Written in 1741, Edwards's sermon describes us sinners as spiders the Creator dangles over the mouth of hell. "The wrath of God burns against them, their damnation does not slumber, the pit is prepared, the fire is made ready, the furnace is now hot, ready to receive them, the flames do now rage and glow." I love this sermon as literature because its diabolical lingo is so grim, so harrowing that it's almost cute. Wasn't so cute in yesteryear. Valesky says, "Your first definition of you as a woman, me as a man is that we are sinners. You are a sinner. I'm a sinner. You look at

God. What are you seeing? An angry god—'Sinners in the Hands of an Angry God.' "

Valesky says that thinking about that sermon and its notion that human beings are arachnids God is about to flip into a fire helps him understand that the ways of the Oneida Community, in which heaven is already here, "was like this incredible shot of oxygen. Because we're not so evil. That is behind us. God doesn't have to be angry."

Interesting. I have this recurring nightmare in which I have to move back in with my old college roommates. I'll admit, that's what I was expecting to find at Oneida—the nineteenth-century equivalent of sharing a house with the friend who brought home a crazy drifter to sleep on our couch, a man who claimed the local car dealership was built out of "needles nourishing the earth." The week before I went to Oneida I had that claustrophobic dream again, that I had to move back in with the girl who claimed to enjoy baking and always promised tomorrow was going to be muffin day even though tomorrow was never muffin day—it was muffin day maybe once. But Valesky inspired me to think about the claustrophobia of American culture in the eighteenth and nineteenth centuries, how women like me would have given anything for a freewheeling life with Drifter Magnet and Muffin Day instead of being doomed to a choice between Mother Superior and Husband Your Parents Picked. How reassuring it must have been to have this place, to know that it was here. If I had never gone to Oneida and talked to Joe Valesky, if I had simply read a book about the community and bought my Oneida teapot at Macy's Herald Square, I might have thought about fornicating utopians as I brewed Earl Grey, but now, when I watch the steam rise from the yellow spout, I like to pretend I'm seeing people breathe.

*

When James Garfield, the Republican Party's presidential nominee, left the 1880 convention to return to his farm in Mentor, he was under the impression that he was running against Democrat Winfield Scott Hancock. His true opponent, however, was his fellow Republican, Senator Roscoe Conkling. Garfield had barely been home long enough to hire extra help for his beet harvest when Conkling was summoning him to New York for a meeting of the Republican National Committee.

"I am very reluctant to go," Garfield complained to his diary on July 28, 1880. "It is an unreasonable demand that so much effort should be made to conciliate one man." But New York was 1880's battleground state. Garfield couldn't win without New York and he couldn't win New York without Conkling. So, for the good of the party, he swallowed his pride and reserved a room at the Fifth Avenue Hotel.

The Fifth Avenue Hotel, on the corner of Twenty-third, housed the New York Republican Party headquarters. It was there Chester Alan Arthur kept his office. It was there the party faithful assembled throughout the 1880 campaign, including the eccentric political gadfly Charles J. Guiteau. The building was torn down in 1908. These days, the site is home to the International Toy Center. A plaque noting the location's former glory is all that's left of Garfield and Arthur.

The hotel would become famous, if you can call anything related to Garfield famous, as the site of the Fifth Avenue

Summit, a private meeting among Garfield and various squabbling Stalwarts, including Roscoe Conkling's lieutenants, VP nominee Chester Arthur and New York's junior senator, Tom Platt. What the men agreed to has been lost to history. Three things, however, are clear: Garfield left the room believing he had not mortgaged his future to the Stalwarts, the Stalwarts left the room believing Garfield had agreed to let them control the Treasury appointment in the cabinet (and thus the almighty New York Custom House), and Roscoe Conkling had the audacity to never step foot in the room at all. At the end of the day, Garfield's diary reports, "The absence of Senator Conkling gave rise to unpleasant surmises as to his attitude. His friends were embarrassed and somewhat indignant." In other words, Conkling commanded the future commander in chief to New York so as to boss him around and then, though Conkling was staying in the same hotel, he didn't have the courtesy to boss Garfield around in person.

Years later, statues of Chester Arthur and Roscoe Conkling were erected across the street in Madison Square Park. Arthur, who became president after Garfield's assassination, is designated as President Chester Alan Arthur on the base of his monument so as to jog the memory of the joggers passing by—Chester who? Conkling's statue, by comparison, wears no such name tag. "Roscoe Conkling" is all that's chiseled at his feet, as if to taunt, "Don't you know who I am?" He ran this town, this state, the whole country sometimes, and now, standing catty-corner from a Dunkin' Donuts, the only attention he is paid is from the dogs and drunks peeing at his granite shoes.

Garfield, more than anyone, would get a kick out of

Conkling's twenty-first-century anonymity. On the other hand, Conkling would be similarly delighted with the dimming of Garfield's star. Conkling's convention speech for Ulysses S. Grant—the one right before Garfield's ode to calm seas—correctly prophesied that Grant's famous name would outlive every man in the room. Conkling would have loved the colossal domed monstrosity uptown known as Grant's Tomb, especially compared to the dinky New York City Garfield remembrances—a tree planted in a cemetery in Queens (it died) and a playground in Brooklyn's Prospect Park with the dignified name Garfield Tot Lot, which my friend Kate, a Park Slope mother of two, describes as "cute but uninspiring."

*

Just for fun, I decided to take a self-guided walking tour of Garfield's Washington, D.C. The prospect is more titillating than one might think, in that to stroll the nation's capital in search of Garfield sites, most of which are either unmarked or torn down, is to feel as if I know a secret. Though, as Washington secrets go, knowing where Charles Guiteau bought his handgun isn't in the same league as Deep Throat's identity. It's just a small, pleasant buzz to amble around and watch the city come alive with forgotten men.

As good a starting place as any is the corner of Pennsylvania Avenue and Seventh Street, at the equestrian statue of Garfield's Democratic opponent in the 1880 presidential election, Winfield Scott Hancock. The bronze Union general grasps binoculars and stares across Pennsylvania at the National Archives' backside. A homeless man in a soiled blanket reclines on the statue's base.

Staring up at Hancock is a handy way to ponder the swampy subtleties of Gilded Age presidential politics. Of the six presidents elected after Andrew Johnson finished serving out Lincoln's second term, five of them—Grant, Hayes, Garfield, Harrison, and McKinley—were Union veterans of the Civil War. Only President Grover Cleveland, who, coincidently, dedicated this monument to Hancock in 1896, did not serve. (He paid a Polish immigrant $150 to replace him in the draft.) The lingering resentment about the Civil War would not fade as an election issue until after McKinley, the last Civil War vet president, militarily reunited North and South for the first time to join forces against Spain in Cuba in the Spanish-American War of 1898.

In the 1880 election, however, 1865 wasn't so much history as news. The Northeast and Midwest, largely Republican, controlled the Electoral College and thus the election—Garfield trounced Hancock there 214–155. But in the popular vote, Hancock lost by a mere ten thousand ballots, which says something about his appeal.

Hancock was a crafty idea for a Democratic nominee. Here was a Democrat who was one of the most beloved, admired Union generals. He fought at Antietam, Fredericksburg, Chancellorsville, and most notably at Gettysburg, where he was wounded, leading the fight that staved off Pickett's charge. (This Hancock statue does adhere to Civil War sculptural tradition in that one of the horse's hooves is raised, which indicates the rider was wounded in battle.) Garfield, by comparison, though a Union general of mild distinction, had actually resigned from the army (with Lincoln's blessing—he needed friendly congressmen) to run for the House of Representatives in 1863.

Republicans thought of themselves *as* the Union, which is to say *as* the United States. One would be tempted to assume that pitting Garfield against a fellow Union general of greater merit might ward off the inevitable post–Civil War Republican campaign tactics of "voting how you shot"—that the old saw about a vote for the Democrats being a vote for reviving the old Confederacy would not, in Hancock's case, wash. Wrong. Even though Hancock was a Pennsylvanian, even though he was known as a hero of Gettysburg, even though he had in fact overseen the execution of the Lincoln assassination conspirators in 1865, his Yankee reputation was rebelled-up considerably in 1867–68 when, commanding Reconstruction Texas and Louisiana, he was mercifully soft toward his fellow local Democrats, which is a nice way of saying he conspired to impede black suffrage and return ex-Confederate whites to political power. Being a defender of the North who was lenient to the South made Hancock an attractive candidate in the biggest battleground state— New York. Democratic-leaning New York City especially had always been ambivalent at best about the Union cause, a fact embodied in the infamous draft riots of 1863, a bloody rebellion against what citizens saw as Lincoln's greed for bodies—theirs.

All of the above makes the Republicans' strategy in 1880 more interesting in that they blatantly ignored Hancock's Civil War bravery. Take, for example, Garfield's campaign song, "If the Johnnies Get into Power." Set to the tune of "When Johnny Comes Marching Home" it goes:

Jeff Davis's name they'll proudly praise, ah ha, ah ha
And Lincoln's tomb will be disgraced, ah ha, ah ha

The nation's flag will lose its stars
The stripes they'll change to rebel bars
And we'll all wear gray if the Johnnies get into power

In other words, a vote for Hancock and the Democrats is a vote against the Republicans, which is a vote against the United States.

That song, by the way, is very Stalwart, which is to say very Conkling, very Grant. One of the slight variances between the Stalwarts and their fellow Republicans the Half-Breeds is that the Half-Breeds, partly out of frustration with the Civil War sainthood of Grant, were clean-shirt guys more interested in stumping for mild civil service reform—a platform whose merit would make for a less stirring campaign song. *A bureaucrat should pass a test, hurrah, hurrah!*

Obviously, the Republican tactics worked. Garfield and Arthur won the election. I stroll south from Hancock's statue toward the Mall. The Capitol looms to the left. It was there on the East Portico, on March 4, 1881, that the new president delivered his inaugural address.

Garfield had been tinkering with the speech for weeks, but he was still up all night the night before working on it. It is generally grand and solemn, with an admirable pledge to ensure black suffrage and an interesting mention of building a canal somewhere in Central America (a Republican goal not met until the administration of Theodore Roosevelt dug across Panama). But Garfield lets loose a few obstinate hints of spark and spite that suggest the old soldier still had some fight in him. He puts the Mormon Church on notice, allowing that while religious freedom will be defended, liturgical outfits breaking the law to practice bigamy in the name of theology will be legally dealt with. There is a seemingly innocuous section on the need for civil service reform, all the more hilarious considering that all night long, as Garfield tried to scratch out the final draft of the address, civil service reform's archenemy, Senator Roscoe Conkling, was hovering in Garfield's hotel room haranguing him about political appointments until the sun came up. Garfield must have giggled jotting down the admonition to remember that political offices "were created, not for the benefit of incumbents or their supporters, but for the service of the Government," all the while Conkling was camped out oblivious, yakking about his preferences for the cabinet and the New York Custom House.

Now we're on the south side of the Mall. Next door to the gloomy Smithsonian castle, the Arts and Industries building is a redbrick Victorian. The museum is currently closed for two years of renovations. I squint through the front doors. Though the ceiling is masked behind some sort of plastic sheeting, the marble tile floor is uncovered, and the bright botanical decorative panels are still cheering up the walls. Compared to the funereal marble of other Greek Revival government buildings around here, Arts and Industries is welcoming and quaint and decidedly unsenatorial.

A plaque to the left of the front door announces that the building was designated a National Historic Landmark in 1977 because "this site possesses national significance in commemorating the history of the United States of America." No clue is given as to what that significance might be.

In his diary, Garfield was about as vague describing what

was surely one of the most important nights of his life. It merits one sentence: "Inaugural reception at Museum building in the evening."

Garfield's inaugural ball was also the building's inaugural event. The new president had been on the Smithsonian's board. As a congressman in 1879, Garfield helped appropriate $250,000 to build this, then known as the National Museum. According to the Smithsonian, "The building was completed in 1881, on schedule and within budget. Per square foot, it was the cheapest permanent government building ever built. It had 80,000 square feet of exhibition space." Eventually, as the other Smithsonian museums sprouted along the Mall, the institution turned this building into administrative offices. (When I was a twenty-three-year-old Smithsonian intern, this is where I reported to get my I.D. badge.)

Looking through the glass at the silent rotunda, I find it hard to picture it as it must have looked on the night of Garfield's ball: decorated with flags and bunting, seven thousand people lit by the glow of three thousand gaslights. But on temporary wooden flooring where the black, brown, and white squares now lie, James A. Garfield danced with his wife. It would be one of their last waltzes. By the time this, the U.S. National Museum, opened its exhibits to the public the following October, Garfield would be dead.

Backtracking across the Mall to Sixth and Constitution—the back entrance of the National Gallery of Art—is where Garfield got shot. This museum building wasn't erected until 1941. Before that, it was the site of the Baltimore & Potomac Railroad station. James A. Garfield walked in here on July 2, 1881. He was carried out on a stretcher.

No plaque marks the spot where Guiteau gunned down Garfield—zip.

I am pro-plaque. New York is lousy with them, and I love how spotting a plaque can jazz up even the most mundane errand. Once I stepped out of a deli on Third Avenue and turned the corner to learn I had just purchased gum near the former site of Peter Stuyvesant's pear tree. For a split second I had fallen through a trapdoor that dumped me out in New Amsterdam, where in 1647 the peg-legged Dutch governor planted a tree he brought over from Holland; until a fatal wagon accident, it bore fruit for more than two hundred years. To me, every plaque, no matter what words are inscribed on it, says the same magic informative thing: Something happened! The gum cost a dollar, but the story was free.

Therefore, it bothers me that an educational edifice like the National Gallery of Art, which, as the name suggests, is operated by the federal government, fails to commemorate the site of a presidential assassination. Especially considering that once, on vacation in Ireland, I noticed the city of Dublin summoned the wherewithal to erect a plaque on a coffee shop celebrating the place as the site where Bob Geldof wrote the song "Rat Trap." And "Rat Trap" wasn't even the Boomtown Rats' biggest hit.

So here's my paper Garfield plaque. On July 2, Garfield was in the sort of jolly good mood enjoyed by anyone about to escape the inferno that is a Washington summer. Accompanied by his sons Hal and Jim and Secretary of State James G. Blaine, Garfield was on his way out of town, first to attend the graduation ceremony at his alma mater, Williams College, followed by a vacation in Long Branch on the New

Jersey shore; Mrs. Garfield, whose malaria made sweaty D.C. especially unbearable, was already in Jersey, enjoying the sea air. (The president had already accompanied his wife to Long Branch earlier in the summer, returning to the White House to work. In fact, even then Charles Guiteau was stalking Garfield at this station as he and Lucretia departed for that trip, but Guiteau later confessed he could not bring himself to shoot the president with his sickly wife looking on. He had chatted with her at a White House reception and liked her.)

Guiteau fired two shots. The first one grazed Garfield's arm. Guiteau lunged forward, pulled the trigger again, aiming at his victim's back. Garfield fell. Guiteau fled toward Sixth Street. A D.C. police officer, having heard two shots, grabbed the assassin and took him into custody.

The wounded president was moved onto a mattress, his head held in the hands of a washroom attendant. But, as Laurie Anderson once put it, "It's not the bullet that kills you, it's the hole." Garfield might have survived the shooting but for what happened next. Namely, that various physicians summoned to the scene, especially Dr. D. W. Bliss, searched for the bullet's location in Garfield's back by poking their grimy fingers into the wound, rooting around in the presidential innards. This despite the advances and inroads of Joseph Lister and his soon-to-be-popular theories about germs. Besides his plea of insanity, Guiteau would in fact capitalize on this medical bungling at his defense trial, arguing that the doctors killed Garfield, "I just shot him."

One witness to the event, who was at the station to see off his boss, was Secretary of War Robert Todd Lincoln, son of the late president. Seeing the shooting would have been traumatic for anyone, but Lincoln, who shuddered for the bleeding president, must have cringed further for Hal and Jim Garfield, the president's sons. Lincoln, remembering the death of his own father a few blocks away sixteen years before, confided to a reporter, "How many hours of sorrow I have passed in this town."

Robert Lincoln, by the way, would continue to run the War Department for Garfield's successor Chester Arthur. In the 1880s, this mostly entailed managing the dwindling Indian Wars out west, with one ghastly exception. The same week Garfield was shot, one of Lincoln's charges, a twenty-five-man Arctic scientific expedition, was en route to Lady Franklin Bay. Robert Todd Lincoln, writes Leonard F. Guttridge in *Ghosts of Cape Sabine*, "could not have cared less about the North Pole." Underprovisioned, thanks mostly to Lincoln's indifference toward the project, the men arrived in the North Pole and set up a base, expecting a relief ship the following year. It never came. After two years went by without supplies or rescue, the starving party abandoned their camp and retreated home. Only six survived. The survivors ate the dead men. It was a fiasco of planning and leadership, a national embarrassment and disgrace, and as the bureaucrat in charge, Robert Lincoln had frozen blood on his hands. When the rumors of cannibalism surfaced, Lincoln and his counterpart the secretary of the navy conspired to cover it up by announcing that the reason the bones of the dead had been mangled by knives was that the survivors cut up their comrades' flesh to use as "shrimp bait." That's how ugly the scandal was—that turning human flesh into shrimp bait was the positive spin.

*

The Smithsonian's National Museum of American History has a handful of Garfield assassination mementos on display in the third-floor presidential exhibit. The very tile from the train station floor, the one Garfield was standing on when Guiteau shot him, was "donated in 1909 by James Garfield, son of the president." It is surprisingly colorful, a mosaic in beige, black, white, brown, blue, and pink that wouldn't be out of place in a baby's room. (Omitted is word on the identity of the ghoul who gave the tile to Garfield junior in the first place.)

In the same display case, a desk calendar belonging to the president ominously rests on the number 2, as "the date has not been changed from the day he was shot." Also nearby: a railroad spike from the special spur built to transport the ailing president to the Jersey shore where he went to recuperate, one of the "valued souvenirs sold to a public desperate for any tangible remembrance of the fallen leader," and a quotation from soon-to-be-president Chester Arthur insisting, "I am an American among millions grieving for their wounded chief."

Rounding out this alcove of presidential death are displays devoted to the Lincoln and Kennedy assassinations; the attempt on the life of Theodore Roosevelt, including the bullet-dinted page of the speech he insisted on delivering after getting shot; and the mourning for the sudden death of FDR. Poor William McKinley, assassinated in 1901, does not warrant a display of his own, only a mention in an exhibit devoted to a brief history of the Secret Service, which contains, said one teenage boy to another, "Dude, guns!" By contrast, thanks to the generous lenders at Planet Hollywood, actor Harrison Ford's presidential suit from the movie

Air Force One does get its very own Harrison Ford–sized display case, with a text panel explaining, "The bloodstain and tear are a result of the movie's fight scenes," I guess because otherwise, a visitor might wonder if a Planet Hollywood patron had accidentally smeared it with ketchup.

*

Near the corner of Fifteenth Street and E, little generals are crawling all over the monument to General William Tecumseh Sherman, commanding their moms. All action halts as a squirrel with a napkin in its mouth circles the statue; it's hard to explain why a squirrel with a napkin in its mouth is riveting, but it is.

I take a seat on one of the benches to consider the weird relief sculptures carved beneath Sherman and his horse. One depicts Sherman and perhaps the same horse in the woods, the general staring at some vague shirred thing that is either a rock or an eagle, unless it's a burning bush. The other panel shows an allegorical female figure who looks like she's playing cat's cradle with the bandages she might have ripped off the dead private whose privates she's standing on.

A little boy slumps onto the bench next to me, accompanied by two adult male guardians, probably his father and his uncle.

"Who's that?" one of the grown-ups asks, nodding up at Sherman.

The kid considers this. He looks at the general, then at the horse, proudly concluding, "It's Paul Revere!"

"Oh," the grown-up replies.

Oh? That's it? No corrections? No "What the heck are they teaching you in school?" Not even an encouraging

"Good guess, but actually . . ."? Besides the fact that even a person speeding past in a cab would recognize Sherman for his punky hairdo alone, if one of these lazy guardians got up off the bench and walked about three and a half feet he could see Sherman's name chiseled there big. Maybe the men are too tired to fact check. But still, this town is lousy with equestrian statues—General Sheridan at Sheridan Circle, General McPherson in McPherson Square, Andrew Jackson, George Washington, etc. If no one corrects this kid he is going to go back home under the impression that Paul Revere is the most important American who ever lived because why else would they erect his statue every two blocks?

"Not that I was eavesdropping," I say, "but that is not Paul Revere. That is General Sherman."

"Oh," says the same guy who said the same thing about Paul Revere. The boy glares at me as if he's wishing I'd get trampled under the hooves of Paul Revere's horse.

Between the hair and the stare, the Sherman monument does convey how ominous Sherman must have been. Which makes Charles Guiteau's note to Sherman, found at the train station not far from Garfield's bleeding body, all the more remarkable, because in the note, Guiteau has the nerve to tell William T. Sherman what to do. Guiteau wrote:

To General Sherman:

I have just shot the President. I shot him several times, as I wished him to go as easily as possible. His death was a political necessity. I am a lawyer, theologian and politician. I am a Stalwart of the Stalwarts. I was with General Grant and the rest of our men, in New York during the canvass. I am going to the jail. Please order out your troops, and take possession of the jail at once.

Very respectfully,

Charles Guiteau

I have seen Guiteau's original note. It resides across town in the Charles J. Guiteau Collection at the Georgetown University Library. Guiteau carried it in his pocket, and the original folds are still visible in the paper. Guiteau's flowery script bears little indication of madness. In fact, it's downright grandmotherly.

Guiteau purchased the gun he used to shoot Garfield just up the street from the Sherman statue, on the corner of Fifteenth and F. He splurged on a handsome bulldog revolver because he imagined that someday, that particular weapon would look good in a museum. (The gun was lost though—the train station tiles notwithstanding, Garfield stuff wasn't as obsessively cared for as Lincoln mementoes.)

The building where Guiteau bought his weapon has been torn down. A commercial building of shops and offices called Metropolitan Square stands there now. On the corner of Fifteenth and F, there are two plaques—one enumerating the many historical events that occurred on the site, and another one picturing the street as it looked in the early nineteenth century, with women in bonnets milling about next to a horse-drawn carriage in front of the Rhodes Tavern, a building erected here in 1799 that was torn down in 1984. According to the plaque's long list, the tavern, among other things, hosted the first city election in 1802 and witnessed "every inaugural parade from Thomas Jefferson's in 1805 until Ronald Reagan's in 1981." Then, in its wonderfully, obviously spiteful closer, the plaque's list ends, "Ballot initiative to preserve the building approved by Washington citizens, 1983. Razed, 1984." What's not to admire about that kind of civic grudge?

There is no mention of Guiteau and his gun, not that there should be. In fact, according to a 1999 article in the *Washington Times* published before the plaque was hung, one of the plaque putter-uppers comes right out and says Guiteau and the gun shop that was here will be omitted from the list.

In the seven or so minutes it takes me to copy down the full text of the verbose plaque—I left out the parts about the congressional boardinghouse and the three years the Washington Stock Exchange was based here—something curious happens. Even though the corner of Fifteenth and F is hardly a tourist hot spot, the fact that I am staring at this obscure, out-of-the-way plaque taking notes attracts five separate families of tourists, who are suddenly elbowing me aside to videotape the plaque. Someone's fitful son slams into my arm, jerking my pen and messing up my notes. "Sorry," his mom whimpers, yanking him off the sidewalk. One dad reads aloud to a couple of children who are neither tall enough to see nor old enough to read that the Riggs Bank was here from 1840 to 1884, because kids love to know where banks used to be.

I have a strange sensation I can't put my finger on. Suddenly it registers. I think I might be crowded. This is a new development in Garfield pilgrimage—other pilgrims.

I stroll over to Lafayette Park to get some air, plunking down on a bench across from the White House, just like Charles Guiteau used to do. Crooking my neck left I can also see the Court of Claims, where Secretary of State James G. Blaine's house used to be. (It was also Secretary of State Seward's house before Blaine, the one in which he was stabbed in the Lincoln assassination conspiracy.)

Upon arriving in Washington from New York, Guiteau dropped by the White House every day begging to be appointed ambassador to France. In his diary, Garfield's annoyance at the throngs of office seekers is weirdly prophetic given the violence to come, complaining of "the indurate office seeker who pursues his prey with the grip of death . . . as highway men draw pistols." He also confesses that it will be "some trouble to keep from despising them." Three weeks before the assassination, which is to say three weeks into his administration, the beg-a-thon has clearly taken its toll. Garfield laments, "Once or twice, I felt like crying out in agony of my soul against the greed for office, and its consumption of my time. My services ought to be worth more to the government than to be thus spent." He goes on to fear that this and all the other presidential hogwash will mentally "cripple" him, wondering, "What might a vigorous thinker do, if he could be allowed to use the opportunities of a Presidential term in vital, useful activity? Some civil service reform will come by necessity, after the wearisome years of wasted Presidents have paved the way for it." On that last point, he was wrong, as his successor, Chester Arthur, would sign a civil service reform bill into law, partly as a Garfield memorial.

Garfield's secretary, no doubt exasperated by the persistent kook Guiteau, had pawned off Guiteau on Secretary of State James G. Blaine, explaining to Guiteau that the French ambassadorship would be decided at the State Department over at the Old Executive Office Building around the corner. Not that Blaine suffered Guiteau for long. On May 14, having had enough of the scruffy oddball who actually believed he deserved one of the cushiest appointments in the history of diplomacy, Blaine screamed at him, "Never speak to me again on the Paris consulship as long as you live!"

Guiteau fired off a letter to the White House describing Secretary Blaine as a "wicked man." He told the president, "You ought to demand his immediate resignation. Otherwise, you and the Republican party will come to grief."

Meanwhile, Garfield took a stand on the most controversial appointment of all, the collector of the New York Custom House. Defying New York senator Roscoe Conkling, Garfield chose William H. Robertson, a seemingly neutral choice. Conkling, however, exploded. Here's what happened. Conkling threatened to block Robertson's Senate confirmation. Garfield pressed the other senators to back his nominee or forsake White House support for the rest of his term. Feeling the political wind blow toward Garfield, Conkling outrageously resigned from the Senate so he didn't have to be there when Garfield won. Conkling forced his fellow New York senator, Tom Platt, to follow suit and resign too. Robertson was confirmed. Meanwhile, Conkling and Platt took the train to Albany, planning to get reappointed by the state legislature—senators weren't popularly elected until 1913—and to return to Washington spoiling for revenge. However, in the Albany hotel where they were staying, ex-senator Platt was spotted entering his hotel room with a lady, a hotel room with a transom over the door in a hotel where many of his political enemies were also staying, one of whom spied the tryst-in-progress and invited all his buddies to take turns peeping in on Platt. Neither Platt nor his comrade Conkling was reappointed to the Senate. (Though Platt would eventually rise from the ashes, reenter the Senate, filling Conkling's shoes as boss of New York. In fact, it was Platt's idea, in 1900, to get New York's annoying governor out of his hair by having him neutered, which is to say nominated for vice president, never predicting that President McKinley would be assassinated less than a year later, making Theodore Roosevelt president of the United States.)

Garfield's diary simply states, "In the war of Conkling versus the administration I have been strengthened in the public judgment." Which is a nice way of saying, "Nyah nyah nyah nyah nyah nyah." Garfield was right, though. The voters did appreciate Garfield standing up to boss rule. The Republican Party, on the other hand, was in turmoil. The Stalwarts were disgraced.

Garfield humiliated the Stalwart faction just as the Stalwart Charles Guiteau's diplomatic dreams were dashed. Guiteau, ever resourceful, found a new reason for being, a moment of clarity born of divine inspiration. God told him to kill the president. In his "Letter to the American People," written on June 16 and found in his pocket when he was arrested on July 2 at the train station, Guiteau explains:

I conceived of the idea of removing the President four weeks ago. Not a soul knew my purpose. I conceived the idea myself. I read the newspapers carefully, for and against the administration, and gradually the conviction settled on me that the President's removal was a political necessity, because he proved a traitor to the men who made him, and thereby imperiled the life of the Republic. At the late Presidential election, the Republican party carried every Northern State. Today, owing to the misconduct of the President and his Secretary of State, they could hardly carry ten Northern States. They certainly could not carry New York, and that is the pivotal State.

Where did Guiteau get his insane notions? Think back to the Republican platform in Garfield's presidential campaign. Guiteau, in his own off-key way, is merely covering that inflammatory campaign song "If the Johnnies Get into Power." So Garfield is the victim of Guiteau, but he's also the victim of his own party rhetoric of exaggerating a Democratic victory into a matter of life and death. Guiteau took these exaggerations to heart, explaining in his letter that while he had "no ill-will to the President" as a person, the president has "wrecked the once grand old Republican party." He continues,

> This is not murder. It is a political necessity. It will make my friend Arthur President, and save the Republic. I have sacrificed only one. I shot the President as I would a rebel, if I saw him pulling down the American flag. I leave my justification to God and the American people.

After God commanded Guiteau to kill Garfield, it actually took the assassin a couple of weeks to summon the nerve to pull the trigger, and all that time he tracked the movements of the president and his friends and family, hunting him. Then Guiteau would go down to the banks of the Potomac to practice shooting by aiming at rocks and trees.

The night before the assassination, Guiteau watched Garfield leave the White House and walk alone to Blaine's house. After a while, the president and the secretary of state left the house together. At his trial, Guiteau, who was spying on them from Lafayette Park, remembered they were "in the most delightful and cozy fellowship possible; just as hilarious as two young girls." It's a pretty picture—nice that Garfield enjoyed the last walk he'd ever take.

Normally, Lafayette Park is one of my favorite spots in town. I like the Marquis de Lafayette and his statue, like thinking about William H. Seward. Sometimes I even like looking at the White House, depending on whose house it is. But sitting where Guiteau stalked Garfield, staring at the White House gives me the creeps. So I take off.

Onward and over to Logan Circle, to the General Logan monument. Yet another equestrian job, this one on its eastern side boasts the lone D.C. sculptural representation of President Chester Alan Arthur. Arthur administers the senatorial oath to the old general; seven others even more forgotten than Arthur (if that's possible) stare on.

Arthur was mortified that Garfield's assassin claimed that he did it so Arthur could be president. As Garfield lay dying, Arthur cringed, hiding out in his Manhattan house on Lexington Avenue, embarrassed and scared. Out of tact, he wanted to avoid the impression that he was taking over the administration but also to allay suspicions that he conspired with Guiteau.

I have some sympathy for Arthur. For starters, he never wanted to be president, and then to have to assume the presidency all because some lunatic Arthur barely noticed hanging around Republic HQ during the campaign killed Garfield on his behalf. Later that evening, after I got home from the Logan monument, I listened to a friend's voice mail telling me that he was listening to the radio and the radio host described the current president as the worst president of all time, except for maybe Chester Arthur, and my friend wanted to know if that was true. I e-mailed him back that actually, Chester Arthur wasn't so bad, unless you were Chinese (he limited immigration). He signed a civil service bill into a law. Plus, after Garfield's death, Arthur's old pal ex-senator Conkling swooped in and, unbelievably, commanded Arthur to fire Garfield's customs collector! Arthur was appalled and said no. The two men would never speak again, though in New York City their statues have to stare wordlessly across Madison Square Park at each other in perpetuity.

(You can learn even more about how Arthur is or is not remembered by stopping by his Lexington Avenue house, where he took the presidential oath the day Garfield died. The moment does warrant a plaque, though not necessarily a plaque people are supposed to be able to see. The plaque hangs *inside* what is now an apartment building's foyer. If you look hard through the glass security door, you can kind of make out a sign above the mailboxes that says something about Arthur and civil service reform.)

In Washington, the District of Columbia Court Building at 451 Indiana Avenue NW was built as the old city hall, becoming a courthouse in 1873. A statue of Abraham Lincoln, erected three years after his assassination, stands in front of the steps.

Today, the dignified columned structure looks abandoned,

surrounded by a perimeter of chain-link fence. But in 1881–82, this is where Charles Guiteau's murder trial took place.

Guiteau's trial was a sensation—a laugh riot well attended by the ladies of Washington, who packed picnic baskets to catch his act. Newspaper accounts describe the proceedings as a circus. A political cartoon by Thomas Nast in *Harper's Weekly*, entitled "From Grave to Gay," pictured an elfin Guiteau, perched on Garfield's grave in the middle of the courtroom, surrounded by grinning lawyers and jurors. Slogans littering the ground include "Anything for a laugh" and " 'Funny' Insanity by Guiteau."

Appointing himself co-counsel in his defense, Guiteau constantly interrupted his own attorneys, including the beleaguered George Scoville, his brother-in-law. Guiteau repeatedly pointed out that in shooting Garfield he was only carrying out the command of God. Finally, the exasperated prosecutor asked him, "Who bought the pistol, the Deity or you?" Then, after the prosecutor brought up the minor matter of the commandment "Thou shalt not kill," Guiteau asserted that God the Father grandfathered Guiteau past this rule. Guiteau then went on to compare himself to Napoleon, Jesus, the apostle Paul and Martin Luther. Guiteau pointed out that like them, he was "a man of destiny." Guiteau pulled stunts such as lobbying the judge to be able to read aloud his autobiography because it would be an oration on par with Cicero's that "will go thundering down the ages." It was a crowd-pleaser, especially since Guiteau read excerpts from admiring letters received from his fellow lunatics. "No one," he said, "wants to shoot or hang me save a few cranks, who are so ignorant they can hardly read or write. High-toned people"—Guiteau's highest praise—"are saying, 'Well, if the Lord did it, let it go.'"

Except for the dead-serious details of his assassinating President Garfield and being in all likelihood clinically insane, Charles Guiteau might be the funniest man in American history—a guy so relentlessly upbeat, so unfailingly optimistic about his place in the world, so very happy for others lucky enough to have made his acquaintance, such a sunshiny self-important glass-all-full sort of fool that he cannot open his mouth or take out his pen without coming up with one unintentionally hilarious gag after another.

The Garfield assassination is always described, on the rare occasions it is described, this way: James Garfield was shot by a disappointed office seeker who had wanted to be appointed ambassador to France.

It is surprising that Guiteau would go down in history as a "disappointed office seeker," because the adjective "disappointed" implies the guy was capable of registering disappointment. Even though he was, at the time of the assassination, a divorcé, a college dropout, a failed lawyer, preacher, and writer. Even though, during his youthful residence at the sexed-up Oneida Community he was the one guy in a free love commune who could not get laid. When Charles Guiteau looked in the mirror he did not see a raggedy homeless man, a wife beater, a dud. He saw the ambassador to France. He wasn't out of work. No, sir. Charles J. Guiteau was "in the employ of Jesus Christ & Co."

In his musical *Assassins*, Stephen Sondheim plays up the inherent humor in Guiteau's unwarranted self-love and sugary outlook. Compared to Hinckley, a downbeat creep, or the

McKinley assassin Czolgosz, a sad son of immigrants always dragging down the room with laments about the unfairness of factory working conditions, Guiteau is the audience's goal-oriented golden boy who smiles while he sings perky lyrics like "look on the bright side."

During Guiteau's trial, one horrifying but effective stunt by the prosecution involved passing around Garfield's spine, which had been removed during the autopsy. Seeing the president's vertebrae being pawed by the jury made the ladies present cry. But this was an uncharacteristically somber exception. Mostly, the attendees ate up Guiteau's entertaining outbursts. (Everyone except for Harriet Blaine, the wife of Secretary of State James G. She made a point of showing up every day *not* to laugh, out of respect for her late friend Garfield. When the trial ended she wrote of Guiteau, "I want it impossible for that hoarse, cracked voice, ever to raise itself again.")

Scoville mounted a convincing insanity defense, assembling expert witnesses, including a former doctor of Guiteau's who had examined him years earlier right after Guiteau threatened his sister with an axe. Also, Guiteau's own babbling, always eccentric and frequently delusional, reads today like classic crackpot. But in 1882, the insanity defense was new and controversial; add a dead president to the mix and the country's thirst for revenge makes an insanity acquittal all the more unlikely. On January 5, 1882, the jury reached a guilty verdict.

Guiteau appealed, but in May, he was sentenced to hang on June 30. Guiteau was angry at the judge, the jury, the press, the American people, and, not least, President Arthur, whom Guiteau regarded as ungrateful considering that

Arthur owed his pay raise and promotion to Guiteau. Four days before his execution, Guiteau penned a bizarre little play in which "The Almighty" confronts Guiteau's enemies and damns them.

> The Almighty asks the newspapermen, "Why did you hound my man to death?"
> "We did not believe he was your man."
> "No excuse. Go to Hell."

The Almighty interrogates President Arthur as to why he did not pardon "my man Guiteau." When Arthur replies that he thought a pardon would deny him the presidential nomination in 1884, the Almighty tells Arthur, "No excuse, you ingrate! Go to Hell. Heat up Mr. Devil!"

On June 30, Guiteau would hang. An old folk song tells the tale:

> My name is Charles Guiteau, my name I'll ne'er deny.
> I leave my aged parents in sorrow for to die.
> But little did they think, while in my youthful bloom,
> I'd be taken to the scaffold to meet my earthly doom.

That song, "Charles Guiteau," was long-rumored to have been written by Guiteau, and I can see why—the first-person narrative, the boasting line about his name. It wasn't. Probably the myth that Charles Guiteau wrote "Charles Guiteau" comes from the fact that Guiteau did write a song that he chanted from the scaffold right before he was hanged on June 30, 1882. (Guiteau was executed on a scaffold outside the jail on the banks of the Anacostia River, on the site of what is presently the D.C. Armory, next to RFK Stadium, which isn't worth the trouble of a trip Guiteau-wise, though the stadium might have sentimental meaning for fans of the Washington Redskins.)

Before reciting his weird poem, Guiteau said to his death witnesses,

I am now going to read some verses which are intended to indicate my feelings at the moment of leaving this world. If set to music they may be rendered very effective. The idea is that of a child babbling to his mamma and his papa. I wrote it this morning about ten o'clock.

Then, he chanted:

I am going to the Lordy, I am so glad,
I am going to the Lordy, I am so glad,
I am going to the Lordy,
Glory hallelujah! Glory hallelujah!
I am going to the Lordy.
I love the Lordy with all my soul,
Glory hallelujah!
And that is the reason I am going to the Lord,
Glory hallelujah! Glory hallelujah!
I am going to the Lord.
I saved my party and my land,
Glory hallelujah!
But they have murdered me for it,
And that is the reason I am going to the Lordy,
Glory hallelujah! Glory hallelujah!
I am going to the Lordy!

I wonder what I will do when I get to the Lordy,
I guess that I will weep no more
When I get to the Lordy!
Glory hallelujah!
I wonder what I will see when I get to the Lordy,
I expect to see the most glorious things,
Beyond all earthly conception,
When I am with the Lordy!
Glory hallelujah! Glory hallelujah
I am with the Lord.

*

The Garfield Monument, a bronze sculpture by John Quincy Adams Ward, was commissioned by the slain president's old army buddies. It stands at the bottom of Capitol Hill facing the Mall. The sculpture intends to present a late-nineteenth-century vision of dignified classicism. But the first thing a present-day visitor notices is that it's exceedingly gay. A life-size, fully dressed Garfield stands on top of a giant shaft. At the foot of the shaft, at eye level, three skimpily clad male figures recline. Meant to portray three phases of Garfield's life—the student, the soldier, the lawmaker—they could not be hunkier. The soldier is a glistening piece of meat with his shirt off, grasping for his sword. The student is supine, come hither, resting his hand on his face, lounging around reading a book. And Garfield looms over them, like a dirty old man pulling up in his car about to take his pick from a lineup of street hustlers.

That is one interpretation. I looked it up and the Office of the Curator of the Capitol sees the Garfield sculpture this way: "The toe of one shoe projects over the edge of the

base, giving the work a sense of vigor and incipient movement."

President Garfield does have a neighbor, and of course,
it's the man who overshadowed the final year of his life,
Ulysses S. Grant. Grant doesn't get a memorial so much as
a sprawling plaza of praise. The sculptural general turned
president is all movement, where Garfield is, vigorous toe
notwithstanding, still. On horseback, hat about to fly off
from his speed, Grant is blatantly hetero, a giant, a blur. He's
surrounded by his soldiers in battle, by four lions facing
west.

Grant desperately desired the Republican nomination in
1880 and when it went to Garfield, Grant was demoralized.
And so, until Garfield's shooting, Grant did only the bare
minimum to aid his fellow Republican. He deigned to make
a single campaign speech for Garfield (in which he did not
mention Garfield's name). Grant made an appearance for
literally two minutes at a reception for President Garfield in
Long Branch, even though the two men were staying across
the street from each other for days. And, to Garfield's alarm,
Grant divulged to the press the contents of a scolding letter
from Grant to Garfield in which Grant denounced Garfield's
appointment to the New York Custom House, which Grant
saw as a slap in the face for his supporters and therefore
himself.

After the shooting, though Guiteau immediately announced himself as a Stalwart of the Stalwarts, which is to
say a supporter of Grant's, one of Grant's first public comments was to wonder if it was the result of "nihilism," the
newfangled Russian nothingness that had only months earlier gotten Czar Alexander II killed.

Despite all that, however, there is one touching story about Grant that Kenneth Ackerman recounts in his book *Dark Horse*. Lucretia Garfield, who was vacationing in Long Branch when her husband was shot, had only just heard the news when there was a knock on her door. In walked Ulysses S. Grant, who held her hand, told her he had seen the same wound many times in battle and those men had lived. At that moment, all his rivalry, resentment, and bitterness toward the president was forgotten and concentrated into comforting the president's wife.

*

One day in November, my friend Bennett and I drive out to Long Branch, New Jersey, to see where Garfield died. Garfield, remember, was shot on July 2 in D.C. Anyone who has ever spent more than ten minutes in the nation's capital between May and September knows how uncomfortable the former swamp can be, and that's without a bullet in the back. Because President Garfield and his malarial wife were so fond of the vacation town of Long Branch, they and the doctors agreed trading steamy Washington for the sea air was in the president's best interest. "I have always felt," Garfield wrote in his diary, "that the ocean was my friend."

Bennett parks the car near the water and we take an unbearable walk on the beach. I'm guessing that in the summertime, the place is crawling with children and partiers, but today the wind is so truly windy the frozen sea spray slaps us cold.

My only knowledge of Long Branch comes from reading about how it was in the 1880s, when it was the swankiest resort town on the Eastern Seaboard. I don't know what I was

expecting—probably a cross between the Hamptons and Colonial Williamsburg—but the waterfront is a shock. "There
is no evidence of its past charm," announces Bennett. Barren
and blank, it has what he accurately describes as "an Eastern
bloc vibe." A bland concrete hotel that looks like a Soviet
apartment building (and not in a good way) hovers over a
boardwalk scattered with benches, which sounds cordial
enough, except these benches, also concrete, look like you're
supposed to rest on them on the walk home from standing in
a nine-hour bread line while being tailed by the KGB.

Bennett says, "The only thing that's interesting to me
about this place is the fact that it ever once appealed to any-
body. I do find it interesting how a place or a thing or a person changes, loses what it was that once defined it, and how
some struggle to retain the idea of it despite its passing."

He thinks Long Branch is "cursed" and that the "hostile"
windstorm is a warning to me. He advises me to take heed,
because if I ever return, "I'm sure you'll be hit by lightning.
Or perhaps a tidal wave."

On the beach, amidst the communist concrete, standing
where logic dictates the statue of Lenin should be, is a life-
size James A. Garfield staring at the sea. The area is called
Presidential Park. Garfield's statue, his left hand holding a
patina-green hat, watches over a series of benches, each one
dedicated to the presidents who vacationed here and decorated with small portraits and informational tidbits advertising Grant's twelve years of sojourns while pointing out that
Arthur "leased a cottage on Park." This configuration is remarkable if only because it is the one place in the country
where, in a lineup of presidents, Garfield wins. You have to
die here to get a statue; otherwise, have a bench.

Shivering, we get back in the car and turn the heat all the way up, driving a mile or so down the shore to where Garfield died. *Harper's Weekly* ran a poignant illustration of what he looked like in his final days here, propped up in a bed, looking out the window at his friend the water.

Back then, the ritzy neighborhood was called Elberon. Garfield's cottage, along with Grant's, has long since disappeared. But the homes that are here are more gracious and livable than the melancholy slabs up the beach.

The marker about Garfield's death is clearly an afterthought, a little tombstone next to a hedge on the side of a garage. It's possible to see what Garfield saw from his window. You just have to look past a white picket fence.

Across the way, Joan Schnorbus from the Long Branch Historical Association is waiting for us in front of St. James Chapel, where Garfield and the six other vacationing presidents went to church. For that reason, it is known as the Church of the Presidents. It was deconsecrated in 1953 and turned into a historical museum. It's currently closed for renovations, though "renovations" seems too cosmetic a word for what's going on here. The place was falling apart and the foundation has had to be stabilized, the interior gutted.

Joan unlocks the door of the white shingled building. The sanctuary is dark and strewn with piles of junk and rubble. She points at a wicker rocking chair, says it might have belonged to Ulysses S. Grant. "It's kind of a grandma's attic in here."

She says, "Because the church was the primary church for the well-to-do who vacationed here, and Garfield did die across the road, when he passed away they brought him here before they took him back to Washington."

I tell her we just looked at Garfield's death marker and ask if it was the historical association's doing.

"Actually," she says, "it was a twelve-year-old kid. In the late fifties, early sixties, he decided that it should be there and petitioned the local government to put something there."

I say, "It's kind of—"

"Right next to a garage. I know. It's really such a shame. There's so much history in the area. That's why I'm so adamant about this place because this truly is all we've got. Presidential history in Jersey is so sketchy. Cleveland was born here, but left when he was a toddler. And of course we had Washington, but not as a president. So this is the strongest facility we have in terms of presidential history."

At that moment, I become a lot more interested in Joan than I am in the church. She knows about Grover Cleveland's childhood. I ask her how she got interested in such things.

"I like presidential history," she says. "Have since I was a kid."

"Who's your favorite president?"

"Jackson, actually."

"Jackson?" I blurt, "Oh my lord. You know my ancestors were on the Trail of Tears?"

"My god. I'm sorry." She really is. It's endearing. The unforeseen pleasant surprise about traveling around the country researching historical ugliness is that I seem to luck into a lot of present-day kindness, making the acquaintance of an embarrassment of knowledgeable nice people like Joan who are generous with their time, happy to share what they've learned.

"When I was a little subdued kid," she explains, "Jackson

gave me courage. I was nine when I saw a show about him when he was a kid and fought the British. So it's not his politics, it's more that he, when I was timid, gave me strength."

"That's nice you could get something from a genocidal monster," I joke, asking her if she's been to the Hermitage, Jackson's estate outside of Nashville. She has. She was fifteen.

Garfield, stately, starchy Garfield, though in some ways a better man than Jackson, is unquestionably less dramatic. I ask Joan if she was always keen on the president who died here or if it was living in the area that sparked her. The latter, she says. Because I find Garfield such a blurry figure, so hard to get to know, I ask her if she has a sense of who he was. Yes, she's been reading books about him for a while now.

"What's your favorite thing about him?"

"I never thought of it in that vein." Understandable. "I guess his versatility. He was pretty versatile with his teaching, and he's got that military background. I think there would have been more to him had he stuck around. I think we would have gotten more out of him. I know that Grant did not like him."

"No," I agree.

"When Garfield was ill, Grant did go see him here."

"But Garfield had to get shot first." I bring up that story I like, about Grant showing up at Lucretia Garfield's door to comfort her, that I thought that said a lot about Grant's basic decency, that he would go say hi.

"Yes, I think Grant was a good guy basically. And Arthur, a very impressive man, actually, the way he went against—let me think of the word . . . the guys that put him in office?"

"The Stalwarts?"

"Yes, the Stalwarts. Arthur did his own thing. He did not toe the line for them."

I ask Joan about the Long Branch Historical Association's plans for the church. She says they're trying to raise $3 million. They're not only trying to turn it back into a museum. They want it to become a community center, hold concerts and events.

"It really has so much potential," says Joan, looking around. "We could use it for exhibits, weddings, musicals, plays—"

"Bar mitzvahs," Bennett adds.

She points at a huge bell. "It was in the tower. The belfry was so unstable." It's the bell that rang for Garfield when he died.

She takes us outside, shows us the yard, which contains a small shed so cute it is referred to as a teahouse. It looks like dolls would live in it, dolls or teddy bears. Painted red with white trim, it's nailed together out of railroad ties. Specifically, the ties from the dying Garfield's rail spur to the sea.

The citizens of Long Branch, in a moving act of neighborly devotion, volunteered to build a special spur from the train station so as to more comfortably transport the president to his oceanfront cottage. They laid 3,200 feet of railroad track. And when the president's train stalled at the end of its seven-hour journey, the townspeople pushed Garfield's car all the way to its destination by hand. And then, after Garfield's death, after the rail spur was torn out, some sentimental local, someone like Joan, gathered the wood and built a little house out of it.

Souvenir coaster based on the logo for Buffalo's
Pan-American Exposition, where Leon Czolgosz shot
President William McKinley in 1901. The fair aimed to
promote trade and friendship among the United States,
Canada, and Latin America. The Spanish-American
War of 1898 hastened a need for such hemispheric PR,
which is almost laughably illustrated by Miss North
America's bare foot, poised to stomp on Cuba.

CHAPTER THREE

PAN – AMERICAN EXPOSITION · 1901 · BUFFALO · N · Y · U · S · A ·

A few days after my sister Amy got home from the Oneida-to-Canton, Garfield-McKinley dream vacation I roped her and my nephew Owen into, she phoned me, saying, "I asked Owen what he wanted to do today and he said, 'Go look at stones with Aunt Sarah.' Do you know what he's talking about? What these stones are?"

I do. "He means tombstones," I told her. "When you were off parking the car at the cemetery in Cleveland, Owen and I walked around looking for John Hay's grave. Owen climbed on top of it and hollered, 'This is a nice Halloween park!' " (That's what he calls cemeteries.)

James Garfield's tomb stands on top of Lakeview Cemetery's highest hill. Owen calls it "Aunt Sarah's castle." The mausoleum, a colossal Gothic tower completed in 1889, features a chapel, a burial chamber, and stairs opening onto a balcony looking out across Cleveland—the downtown skyscrapers, a gray-blue blotch of haze that might be Lake Erie. From Garfield's perch, trees outnumber the smokestacks. Two individuals can't help but stick out from this view—architect Frank Gehry, whose unmistakable roof wiggles in the distance, and industrialist John D. Rockefeller, whose exclamation point of an obelisk thrusts up a few yards down the hill.

Inside the mausoleum's dome, the liturgical light of stained glass illuminates a larger-than-life-size statue of Garfield. Amy, Owen, and I march downstairs to the burial chamber to look at the flag-draped coffin of James Garfield and the one belonging to Lucretia, his wife. Owen peers closely into every cranny of the room. Frowning, he makes one of his verb-free proclamations, "There no skeletons in the crypt."

Owen is the most Hitchcockian preschooler I ever met. He's three. He knows maybe ninety words and one of them is "crypt"? Amy says, "Remember, Owen? The skeletons are *inside* the coffins."

I have not been particularly shocked by how much I love Owen, but I am continually pleasantly surprised by how much I like him. He's truly morbid. When he broke his collarbone by falling down some stairs he was playing on, an emergency room nurse tried to comfort him by giving him a cuddly stuffed lamb to play with. My sister, hoping to prompt a "thank you," asked him, "What do you say, Owen?" He handed back the lamb, informing the nurse, "I like spooky stuff."

"That was fun, Mama," says Owen as Amy straps him back into his car seat to leave the cemetery. Before we do, I make her drive around for the longest time, trying to locate Mark Hanna's tomb. A little motion sick from winding her way around the hills while scanning for Hanna's name, Amy asks, "Now *who* is this guy?"

I answer that he was an Ohio senator, that as William McKinley's campaign manager in the 1896 presidential election he raised six or seven million dollars when the opponent only scraped together about 600K, that Hanna's nickname was "Dollar Mark," that after he heard about McKinley's assassination and realized Theodore Roosevelt would be sworn in, he's the one who famously quipped, "Now that damn

ASSINATION VACATION

cowboy will be president of the United States," and that the current president's political guru, Karl Rove, claims Hanna as his campaign strategy hero. Hearing this, Amy sighs theatrically, which, in twin language, I understand as a hint that sleazy innovations in election finance and quips about TR are shaky reasons to drag out this car-sickening visit when she would very much like to return to our air-conditioned hotel room downtown for room service and a nap.

I try to sweeten the deal, remembering, "Oh! And Hanna's tomb was designed by Henry Bacon, the architect of the Lincoln Memorial!"

"Wow. Henry Bacon. Yay."

"We'll just wait in the car," Amy says after I spot it. I run up to Hanna's Parthenon, crossing between fluted columns to peek in at Mr. and Mrs. Dollar Mark.

Normally, my sister has bottomless patience for looking at things having to do with the dead people and extinct dinosaurs Owen and I are interested in, but it's been a long day. We've already been to Canton and back, having wasted nearly two hours sidetracked in a mall parking lot where we had stopped for lunch and gotten waylaid by a deranged woman who called the cops, alleging that our rental car was responsible for the apostrophe-size scratch on her Pontiac Grand Am. So Amy had to hash it out with the woman in the back of a patrolman's squad car while Owen and I sat in the hundred-degree heat staring at ants frying on the asphalt, all because I wanted to see the tomb of yet another assassinated Ohio president. (Of course the officer sided with Amy, who, gloating as she got out of the police car, sneered at the Pontiac driver, "My sister is writing a book about our trip and I bet she's going to put you in the McKinley chapter.")

_191_

Like Garfield's, the McKinley National Memorial in Canton is a domed edifice on top of a hill. It's a gray granite nipple on a fresh green breast of grass. A wide staircase connects the mausoleum to the parking lot. Halfway up the stairs, a statue of McKinley stands watch. An inscription describes him as "good citizen, brave soldier, wise executive, helper and leader of men." My guess is that the statue is inspirational for the visitors, but since all of them are joggers bounding past him up the steps and back, up the steps and back, I bet it's McKinley's portly girth more than his good citizenship that inspires them, if only to endure more laps.

Next to the tomb, the William McKinley Presidential Library and Museum displays William McKinley's ice skate; his bank book from 1892–1893, "the period of his personal financial crisis" (from which Mark Hanna bailed him out); photos of McKinley hosting visitors here in Canton during his front porch campaign; an "Iver Johnson .32 caliber revolver identical to the one used by anarchist Leon Czolgosz to assassinate President McKinley in September 1901"; a sullied white nightshirt believed to have been worn by McKinley as he lay dying; and a pair of slippers crocheted by Ida, McKinley's wife.

The McKinley museum displays the silk bag where Ida kept her yarn and knitting needles, complete with a photograph of her dead husband affixed inside. That is how she passed her widowhood. She sewed a picture of her murdered spouse into her knitting bag and then spent the rest of her life in a rocking chair, crocheting four thousand pairs of bedroom slippers, seeing her dead husband's face staring up at her every time she reached for a new ball of yarn.

I think about Ida, the constant looping of her hook

through the yarn, every time I play with my souvenir from the museum that I keep on my desk—the McKinley Memorial yo-yo. It is the only yo-yo I've ever seen decorated with the picture of a mausoleum.

Quarantined on that Canton hilltop, McKinley's tomb is as opulent as it is abstract. It's where his bones are, his skeleton, as Owen would say, but I can't say that looking at his coffin beneath the coffered dome made me feel like he was close.

On the other hand, the simple marker of his assassination on a residential street in Buffalo gets to me. It's just a plaque bolted to a big rock on the ground. You would miss it if you weren't looking for it. Yesterday in Buffalo, we were looking for it and we missed it twice. After Amy has driven up and down Fordham Drive a couple of times without spotting the thing, I finally flag down a dog walker—they seem to know these things—and he points up the block, says it's a few houses in from Lincoln Parkway.

Lined with earthy bungalows, the street is American-dreamy, all sidewalks and green lawns. The McKinley marker sits inside the grassy center median that makes the middle of the road into a long, skinny park. We get out of the car, read the plaque. Sponsored by the Buffalo Historical Society, it says, "In the Pan-American Temple of Music which covered this spot President McKinley was fatally shot Sept. 6, 1901."

At four o'clock that afternoon, McKinley hosted a receiving line, shaking the hands of exposition-goers and kissing babies as an organist played Bach's Sonata in F. One of the people waiting in line was James Parker, a black waiter from Georgia who worked at the fair but had taken the afternoon off to meet the president. In front of him, a man extended his bandaged hand to McKinley. But that was no bandage. The assassin Czolgosz had wrapped his revolver in a handkerchief. When Czolgosz shot McKinley in the stomach the handkerchief caught fire. Czolgosz, who never said a thing, shot McKinley once again. One of McKinley's guards, Private Francis O'Brien, tackled the assassin before he could fire a third shot. Then James Parker punched Czolgosz in the head. O'Brien extracted the gun from Czolgosz's hand. McKinley, who seemed to care less about what the bullets were doing to his insides than what the news of the bullets would do to his notoriously frail wife, told his secretary not to tell her.

All of which took place right here where this marker is. I wonder how many times that dog walker has allowed his pet to pee on it. McKinley's death is part of this neighborhood's life. My dad knows a woman who grew up here, and her brother has had a scar on his face since they were kids; he got it crashing his bike into the rock with the plaque—one of Leon Czolgosz's lesser victims. Hunkered down in the everyday midst of the families on the block, McKinley's death seems more personal and thus more sad, the loss of a husband, a friend. This rock calls to mind Mark Hanna's lament at his dying chum: "William, William, speak to me!"

The architecture of the Pan-American Exposition was built to be torn down. The temporary structures, including the Temple of Music, were modeled out of staff, a kind of plaster reinforced with hemp. The New York Building was the only one they put up for keeps. Now the Buffalo and Erie County Historical Society Museum, it's nice that it's still here but too bad that they saved the one building that's least representative of what the fair looked like. In 1901, the New York Building's marble and columns was a bleached island of Greece in a colorful ocean of colonial Spain.

In fact, the Pan-American Exposition was called "The Rainbow City" to distinguish it from the neoclassical "White City" that was the Chicago World's Fair of 1893. Still, the Pan-American used color as an argument *for* whiteness. In one of the more bizarre manifestations of the turn-of-the-century social Darwinism fad—which employed Darwin's theory of evolution to argue that Anglo-Saxon culture was the fittest and therefore the best, a claim made on stomachs full of steak and kidney pie by men who never tasted the glory that is the taco—the Pan-Am appointed a "director of color" who cooked up a thematic scheme in which "primitive" pursuits and societies' buildings were slathered with summery paint and "civilized" advancements were pastel. Thus, the buildings devoted to horticulture or ethnology (i.e., things growing in dirt and nonwhites living in the dirt) were painted shades of orange, whereas the expo's most important building, the four-hundred-foot-tall Electric Tower, was "ivory-white" with capitalist accents of green and gold.

According to Buffalo attorney and Pan-Am president John G. Milburn, in whose home McKinley would die, the point of the exposition, its guiding principle, was one "grand idea —the bringing closer together of the peoples of this hemisphere in their social, political, and commercial relations. That aspect of it has been the inspiration of the enterprise and the source of the enthusiasm which has carried it forward to completion."

President McKinley had actually come to Buffalo back in

1897 to break ground for an exposition. But something got in the way: 1898. The fair was postponed due to the Spanish-American War. Because of the Cuban combat, the United States was suddenly a world power almost overnight. In fact, during one twenty-four-hour period in August, we conquered Manila Bay in the Philippines *and* seized control of Puerto Rico. McKinley also annexed Hawaii and Guam. So what better way to calm the nerves of our hemispheric neighbors, thought the Buffalo exposition planners, than ask the Latin American and Canadian governments to join us in putting on a show? The exposition's secret theme? *We're Not Going to Shoot You (Especially If You Buy Our Stuff).*

At the Buffalo and Erie County Historical Society Museum, I buy a coaster of the Pan-American's logo, the best possible picture not just of the exposition and its aims of hemispheric friendship, but of the McKinley administration itself. It is an allegorical picture of the Western Hemisphere. North America is a blond woman, South America a brunette. Both of them are white. Swimming between the Atlantic Ocean and the Pacific, the two women clasp hands in friendship. The handshake takes place in Central America on the future site of the Panama Canal. Miss South America smiles, unaware that two years later, the U.S. Navy would swoop in and hack her arm off at the elbow so that cargo ships could sail through the blood of her severed stump.

In the logo, most of the United States and Canada is blanketed in Miss North America's billowy yellow dress. But one delicate bare foot pokes out of the southeastern edge, shaped like the state of Florida, as if she's poised to step on Cuba.

The Cuban people suffered at the hands of the Spanish in the 1890s, especially those who were rounded up into concentration camps. American newspapers, especially Joseph Pulitzer's *New York World* and William Randolph Hearst's *New York Journal,* sensationalized Spanish atrocities, stirring up an idealistic fad for *Cuba libre* among the American people. The clincher, the hard proof of Spanish evildoing was one of those acts that, in retrospect, might not have happened at all. Historians still disagree. On February 15, 1898, the American battleship the *Maine* exploded in Havana Harbor, killing around 260 men. Remember the *Maine*? War boosters like Hearst accused the Spanish of bombing the ship and shrieked for a declaration of war. In fact, the evidence was inconclusive then and remains so today. Some historians believe it may have been a freak accident, a coal fire that ignited explosives on board the ship.

Four days after the *Maine* went down, Hearst called on the public to contribute to the construction of a monument to the fallen in New York. Dedicated in 1913, the *Maine* memorial, a forty-foot-tall tower decorated with allegorical sea people and inscribed with the names of the dead, guards the southwestern entrance to Central Park at Columbus Circle. Nowadays it looks like it was always there; on sunny afternoons citizens sit on or near it, eating sandwiches and watching break-dancers in yellow tracksuits perform acrobatics for spare change. At the time it was erected, the *Maine* memorial was criticized as a park-spoiling monstrosity—a "cheap disfigurement" for which trees were cut down to make room. Like the obnoxious William Randolph Hearst himself, it seemed to take up too much space. Good thing all those people who hated it were dead by the time the eighty-story Time Warner Center went up across the street; that thing makes the hulking *Maine* memorial look like an adorable little birdbath.

And, while we're on the subject of Central Park and McKinley and Hearst, northeast of the *Maine* memorial, up the block from the park's 102nd Street entrance, is a monument to Hearst's most powerful editor and columnist, Arthur Brisbane. A pink granite job with a portrait of Brisbane in profile and a bench to sit on, it lauds Brisbane as "a champion of work and peace before all mankind." Never mind that after the McKinley assassination, Hearst was excoriated for a column he published in the *New York Journal* five months before Leon Czolgosz pulled the trigger, an anonymous column generally attributed to Brisbane that said of the president, "If bad institutions and bad men can be got rid of only by killing, then the killing must be done." Hearst's enemies even spread the erroneous rumor that Czolgosz was carrying that *Journal* clipping in his pocket upon arrest. Hearst, scared for his life, started carrying a revolver. (The publisher lived another fifty years.)

That the *Maine* memorial stares across the asphalt at the Christopher Columbus statue on Columbus Circle is a reminder of just what the United States was up against taking on Spain—the empire of Columbus and Cortés. These people overpowered the Aztecs, took over Holland, parts of Italy, and France. Sure, Spain's power had been on the decline since the Brits trounced its Armada in 1588, but they were so powerful and so rich from the conquistadors' gold, it still took another three centuries to knock them down for good. In 1898, Spain still owned Cuba, Puerto Rico, Guam, and the Philippines, which is to say they controlled Caribbean sugar as well as a couple of handy off ramps to the market of China. It says a lot about American military confidence that this upstart baby of a country was ready to challenge what had once been the mightiest empire since Rome. We had of course won the Revolutionary War against the British, but no one was certain if that marked our beginning as an international force to be reckoned with, or if it was a fluke victory inspired by our willingness to die before we'll pay too many taxes.

Back in 1898, days before the *Maine* blew up, Hearst's *Journal* published a letter attributed to a Spanish diplomat that accused McKinley of being "petty" and "weak." The article's subtle headline: "Worst Insult to the United States in Its History."

At first President McKinley resisted going to war with Spain. The Civil War veteran lamented, "I've been through one war. I have seen the dead piled up, and I do not want to see another."

Then, as now, optional wars are fought because there are people in the government who really, really want to fight them. The Paul Wolfowitz of McKinley's first term, Assistant Secretary of the Navy Theodore Roosevelt, was a part of a group of young wonks from various branches of the government who had been arguing that it was in the American interest to wrench Cuba from the clutches of Spain. They feared what would happen if the unpredictable Cuban rebels governed themselves, they wanted American companies to get a piece of the Cuban sugar business—described as white gold then the way oil is nicknamed black gold now—and they thought Cuba would be a convenient base of

199

operations from which to get cracking on that canal they hoped to one day build in Central America.

Roosevelt wanted all those things, but more than anything, he wanted to fight. He wanted to wear an outfit— I mean, uniform. He wanted—to use one of his favorite words—"adventure." And he wanted these things so badly that once the United States declared war on Spain he resigned as assistant secretary of the navy, ordered himself a custom-tailored uniform from Brooks Brothers, and volunteered to fight as a comparatively lowly lieutenant colonel with the First U.S. Volunteer Cavalry.

Roosevelt helped assemble the volunteer cavalry, a ragtag regiment of cowboys, Indians, Ivy League graduates, one genuine Dodge City marshal, and a Jew nicknamed "Porkchop," that came to be known as the Rough Riders. He described the Rough Riders as men in "whose veins the blood stirred with the same impulse which once sent the Vikings over sea."

And how did our Vikings fare? The war was over in four short months. America's first time out in interventionist warfare with the aim of regime change was seen as such a success that it became known, in John Hay's phrase, as the "splendid little war." Success, hell; if Teddy Roosevelt is to be believed it was downright fun—in his memoir of his Rough Riders days, he can't stop using the word "delighted."

Marking my place in Roosevelt's book, I went to the kitchen to fetch some tea. As I was putting the boiling cup on my desk, I focused on the Pan-American Exposition souvenir coaster I bought in Buffalo, the one with the two female continents holding hands. I used Roosevelt's book as a coaster instead, holding up the Pan-Am logo to get a closer look.

The model for South America was Broadway actress Maxine Elliot. North America, a pretty blonde, was modeled on Maud Coleman Woods of Charlottesville, Virginia. (Sadly, she would die of typhoid fever that summer, ten days before McKinley arrived in Buffalo, thereby never living to see herself on a coaster, every southern belle's dream.)

That North America would be symbolized by a Virginian, by the daughter of a Confederate army captain no less, would have been unthinkable before the Spanish-American War. It was the first conflict in which North and South cooperated after the Civil War.

McKinley and Mark Hanna, already innovators in corporate campaign contributions, were the first Republicans to actively woo white (male) southern Democrats. (The two made a point of vacationing in Thomasville, Georgia—where Hanna's brother Mel had bought a plantation for cheap— in 1895, where they planned the '96 campaign and courted local pols.)

Another milestone in the history of how the party of Lincoln became the party of, say, late South Carolina senator Strom Thurmond, was a Spanish-American War victory speech McKinley delivered to the citizens of Atlanta, praising the Cuban campaign's "magic healing, which has closed ancient wounds and effaced their scars." Later on, McKinley then boiled down the story of the Civil War—on both sides—to merely the story of "American valor" (i.e., doesn't matter which side you were on or what you thought you were fighting for, the point is, you put up a fight). It might be easy to laud these forgiving sentiments as almost Lincolnesque calls for peaceful coexistence, but Lincoln, in his Second Inaugural, was able to ask for reconciliation without lying about what was at stake, without demeaning one of the grisliest moral conflicts in all of history as some silly rite of passage that turned boys into men. Though McKinley and Hanna's ploy was morally questionable, it was nevertheless political genius.

At the Pan-American Exposition, one of the exhibits embodied this revisionist history zeitgeist. It was called the Old Plantation, a celebration of the Old South complete with slave cabins and cotton fields, and featuring a black man billed as "Old Laughing Ben from Dublin, Georgia." Because slavery: fun!

*

Though McKinley hesitated to go to war in the first place, he nevertheless warmed up to the idea of empire. After the U.S. Navy, under the command of Admiral George Dewey, had defeated the Spanish ships in Manila Bay in August of 1898 (with the help of the Filipino rebels who had been attacking the Spanish for years), McKinley debated whether or not to give our Filipino allies their independence or take over the archipelago as an American territory. Addressing some Methodist ministers after the fact, McKinley recalled his decision-making process this way:

> I walked the floor of the White House night after night until midnight; and I am not ashamed to tell you, gentlemen, that I went down on my knees and prayed to Almighty God for light and guidance more than one night. And one night late it came to me this way—I don't know how it was, but it came . . . that we could not leave them to themselves—they were unfit for self-government—and

they would soon have anarchy and misrule over there worse than Spain's was . . . that there was nothing left for us to do but to take them all, and to educate the Filipinos, and uplift and Christianize them, and by God's grace do the very best we could by them, as our fellow-men for whom Christ also died.

Never mind that the Philippines were already largely Christianized, thanks to the Spanish missionaries who arrived in 1565 to convert the Filipinos to Catholicism. Still, these God-made-me presidential war rationales apparently never go out of fashion. In the 2003 State of the Union Address, President Bush—who back when he was governor of Texas confided in a televangelist friend, "I believe God wants me to run for president"—foreshadowed the coming Iraqi war by claiming, "We Americans have faith in ourselves but not in ourselves alone." If you think he is referring to the United Nations, guess again. "We do not know—we do not claim to know all the ways of Providence," he continued, "yet we can trust in them, placing our confidence in the loving God behind all of life and all of history."

When President McKinley delivered the last speech of his life, at the Pan-Am on September 5, 1901, he said, "Expositions are the time keepers of progress." He was alluding to the exhibits devoted to technological advancement—cash registers and mining and hot air balloons, a peculiar building full of infant incubators in which tourists stared at low-birthweight babies as lightbulbs warmed them to health. But it's just as true to see the exposition as a fly trapped in amber, an accounting of American racial attitudes as seen in the ethnological displays—the aforementioned Old Plantation,

"Darkest Africa." There were also fake battles between American Indians and U.S. cavalry staged in the sports arena. (Guess who always won?)

An inscription on the Department of Agriculture Building at the exposition read: "To the ancient races of America, for whom the New World was the Old, that their love of freedom and of nature, their hardy courage, their monuments, arts, legends and strange songs may not perish from the earth." I would imagine that if you were one of the Filipinos employed at the exposition to tend the water buffalo in the Philippine village and you read this slogan, which can be summarized as *we might exterminate you but we'll be sure and put your pottery in our museums,* you might get nervous about current events back home.

The Spanish-American War is often cited as the United States' first interventionist attack on foreign soil. That's only true if you're not counting U.S. wars against the nations of the Sioux, the Nez Percé, the Apaches, the Blackfoot, the Creek, Choctaw, Seminole, Chickasaw, Cherokee, and so on. After God told McKinley to "annex" the Philippines, our former allies the Filipino rebels fought back in a nasty guerrilla war that dragged on for years in which both sides committed torture (the famous "water cure" in which dirty water is poured down a person's throat until he drowns) and atrocities (such as setting buildings on fire with people asleep inside).

Many of the American soldiers and officers who were torturing Philippine rebels (who then tortured them right back) were veterans of the Indian Wars on this continent. On the island of Samar, for example, American troops fought under the command of Wounded Knee alumnus Jacob Smith, who applied skills in the Pacific he had learned slaughtering the Lakota Sioux in South Dakota. After a cunning but brutal ambush by the Filipino guerrillas, Smith ordered his troops to retaliate by shooting to kill every Filipino capable of bearing arms. When asked to pin down a minimum age for the murderees, Smith decided on ten. If it seems distasteful and condescending to read that then-governor of the Philippines William Howard Taft referred to the local citizenry as his "little brown brothers," that's downright sweet compared to what the soldiers called them—"niggers." As one U.S. soldier stationed in the Philippines put it, "The country won't be pacified until the niggers are killed off like the Indians."

Mark Twain had supported the 1898 invasion of Cuba because "it is a worthy thing to fight for one's freedom; it is another sight finer to fight for another man's." But he called the Philippines situation a "quagmire," writing an editorial in the February 1901 issue of *North American Review* called "To the Person Sitting in Darkness." He wrote, "We have stabbed an ally in the back," going on to suggest that a new American flag should be sewn especially for the province "with the white stripes painted black and the stars replaced by the skull and cross-bones."

Leon Czolgosz, confiding in a fellow anarchist not long before he shot McKinley, said of the war in the Philippines, "It does not harmonize with the teachings in our public schools about our flag."

*

When I told a friend I was writing about the McKinley administration, he turned up his nose and asked, "Why the hell would anyone want to read about that?"

"Oh, I don't know," I answered. "Maybe because we seem to be reliving it?"

In 2003 and 2004, as I was traveling around in the footsteps of McKinley, thinking about his interventionist wars in Cuba and the Philippines, the United States started up an interventionist war in Iraq. It was to be a "preemptive war" whose purpose was to disarm Iraqi weapons of mass destruction, weapons which, as I write this, have yet to be found, and which, like the nonexistent evidence of wrongdoing on the *Maine,* most likely never will be. At the outset of the war, President Bush proclaimed that "our nation enters this conflict reluctantly, yet our purpose is sure," just as President McKinley stated, regarding Cuba, "It is not a trust we sought; it is a trust from which we will not flinch." I downloaded the Platt Amendment's provisions toward Cuba from the National Archives' Web site, saw the provision requiring the Cubans to lease land to the United States for a naval base, and then thought about the several hundred Taliban and other prisoners of the War on Terror being held there at Guantánamo Bay. I read a history book describing how McKinley's secretary of war Elihu Root finally—after press uproar sparked Senate hearings—got around to ordering courts-martial for U.S. officers accused of committing the "water cure" in the Philippines, and, closing the book, turned on a televised Senate Armed Services Committee hearing in which Secretary of Defense Donald Rumsfeld was grilled about photographs of giddy U.S. soldiers proudly pointing at Iraqi prisoners of war they had just tortured at the Abu Ghraib prison. I went to NYU to hear former vice president Al Gore deliver a speech calling for Rumsfeld's resignation; Gore asked of the administration's imploding Iraq policy in general and the Abu Ghraib torture photos in particular, "How dare they drag the good name of the United States of America through the mud of Saddam Hussein's torture prison?" Then I walked home through Washington Square Park, where Mark Twain used to hang out on the benches in his white flannel suit when he lived around the corner, and sat down in my living room to reread Twain's accusation that McKinley's deadly Philippines policy has "debauched America's honor and blackened her face before the world."

Looking at the long-term effects of the McKinley administration's occupation of the former Spanish colonies, I can't say I'm particularly optimistic about the coming decades in Iraq. The very fact that we call it the Spanish-American War hints that Cuban sovereignty was a fairly low priority for the McKinley administration. As the Cuban revolutionary hero José Martí worried, "Once the United States is in Cuba, who will drive them out?"

After the United States signed a treaty with Spain in 1898, we occupied Cuba for the next five years. Cuba became nominally independent thanks to an American act of Congress signed into law by McKinley in 1901. It was called the Platt Amendment, but a better name for it might have been "Buenos Dias, Fidel." It kept Cuba under U.S. protection and gave us the right to intervene in Cuban affairs. Which we did for the next half century, reoccupying the country every few years and propping up a series of dictators, crooks, and boobs. The last one, a sergeant named Batista, was one of the monsters created in part by American military aid.

When the revolution came in 1959, all American businesses in Cuba were nationalized without compensation. Yankee, said Castro, go home. And, oh, by the way, how do you like them missiles?

Which is to say: Our failed postwar policy after the Spanish-American War actually led the world to the brink of nuclear annihilation in 1962. And over a century later, Cuba still isn't free.

In the first summer of the Iraqi war, on the crabby, sweaty second day of a blackout that shut down the Northeast's power grid, I stood in line for questionable foodstuffs in my dark neighborhood deli. It reeked of souring milk. An annoyingly upbeat fellow-shopper chirped, "Cheer up, everybody, we're part of history!" Maybe because I was suffering the effects of allergy eyes brought on the night before by trying to read by the light of lilac-scented candles about a political murder committed around the time of the Spanish-American War, I snapped at him. "Sir," I said, "except for the people who were there that one day they discovered the polio vaccine, being part of history is rarely a good idea. History is one war after another with a bunch of murders and natural disasters in between."

*

I happened to be conducting an Internet search for "imperialism and McKinley" when I stumbled onto an editorial in the *Arcata Journal* from the California coastal town of Arcata calling for the local McKinley statue to be torn down because it "represents this nation's dawning season of global militarism, empire-building and corporate-funded, political victories of capitalist classes over working classes, and of racists over reformers." Not only was McKinley getting blamed for the Spanish-American War. In California, they were blaming him for the current one.

After McKinley's assassination, an Arcata resident who had witnessed the president's 1901 speech in San Jose commissioned a San Francisco artist to sculpt McKinley's likeness. The bronze statue survived a foundry fire during the San Francisco earthquake of 1906 and has stood in the town plaza ever since.

In Arcata, President McKinley is the town mascot. At Christmas, the dead president has been known to wear a Santa's hat. Last year, someone broke off his thumb and stole it. According to a report in the weekly *Arcata Eye,* the mayor complained of the theft, "It was a mean, punk-ass thing to do." (The thumb was subsequently recovered and welded back in place.)

I spoke to the *Eye*'s editor, Kevin L. Hoover, who says he moved to Arcata in the first place because of an item in a 1986 issue of the *National Lampoon* reporting that a citizen had stuffed the McKinley statue's nose and ears with cheese.

"I had a pretty horrible job at the time," Hoover recalls. "I said to my best friend, 'Let's go somewhere weird.' I wasn't in journalism at the time, but I came to Arcata and asked around about the cheesing of McKinley. I talked to the actual guy," he says of the fellow who stuffed the cheese. That's when he decided to move there: "It was a place where people stuffed cheese in statues' noses."

I don't know what surprised me more about this town and its statue—that McKinley could be "fun" or that anyone alive was thinking about him at all.

"Arcata is kind of a radical little college town," he continues. (The Green Party has the majority on the city council, for instance.) "Some people here would like to replace the statue with something more politically correct. Every two or three years, a big debate flares up. For some, it's kind of a comic icon. Some people are loyal to it simply because it's always been here. Others just hate it."

One local who would like to tear McKinley down is Hoover's colleague Mark Tide, editor of the *Arcata Journal*. Tide told me he proposes "moving the statue to the deep, right-field corner of our downtown baseball field. There is some logic to such a plan, for McKinley was the first president invited to throw out the first ball of the season." Tide would like to rebuild the gazebo that was in the town square before being displaced by "this bleak, century-long occupation of McKinley."

The *Eye*'s Kevin Hoover admits, "By contemporary standards, McKinley was quite the imperialist bastard. I don't think he was much of a leader. He was a functionary. I like the statue only because he's so irrelevant to Arcata. Why McKinley? Why not Chester A. Arthur instead? Sometimes, there will be some flaming political demonstration with Food Not Bombs and someone will put a picket sign in McKinley's hand."

Even though Hoover is disinclined to ditch the statue that changed his life, I ask him if he finds the opposition to the statue endearing. "Of course," he answers. "There are some very good, principled reasons to get rid of McKinley. The people who want to get rid of the statue think it's an obscenity. We have a real, vigorous diversity of views in our town."

*

There is one thing that the assassinated Americans have in common. Fate seems to grant each man one last good day, some moment of grace and whimsy before he bleeds. (Except, surprisingly, the notoriously good-time JFK, Dallas offering little by way of whimsy.) Lincoln, of course, was giggling at the moment of impact; Booth, knowing the play Lincoln was watching by heart, chose a laugh line on purpose to dampen the noise of his derringer's report. Garfield was jauntily leaving on vacation. Before Robert Kennedy went to the Ambassador Hotel, he spent his last day at the beach with his wife and children at the Malibu home of John Frankenheimer, director of *The Manchurian Candidate*. My favorite, though, is Martin Luther King Jr., who had a pillow fight with his brother and his friends at the Lorraine Motel. I very much enjoy picturing that, and when I do, I see it in slow motion, in black and white. A room full of men in neckties horse around laughing, bonking heads, feathers floating in the air. For William McKinley, it was a day trip to Niagara Falls.

The "Rainbow City" that was the Pan-American Exposition would, come nightfall, turn into the "City of Light." Hundreds of thousands of lightbulbs—forty thousand on the Electric Tower alone—were powered by hydroelectricity generated by nearby Niagara Falls.

So, on the morning of September 6, President and Mrs. McKinley made an excursion to tour the power plant and watch the falls fall. They were delighted. Anyone would be. Amy, Owen, and I went there, took a wet boat ride up close on the *Maid of the Mist*—it was the good kind of terrifying. I would try to describe my awe for the place, but even Steinbeck couldn't think of anything more specific than "Niagara

Falls is very nice." My family and I went to the Canadian side for the better view, a vantage point that was denied President McKinley. In fact, he was very careful not to walk too far across the bridge into Canada because no sitting American president had ever left the country, and he didn't want to stir up a diplomatic hullabaloo. Especially since after the Spanish-American War exposed our lust for sugar, the Canucks might have suspected McKinley was invading to steal their maple syrup.

Thomas Edison's company filmed the Pan-American Exposition. Some of the reels are in the collection of the Library of Congress. In the night scenes of the City of Light, the buildings glow white, as if Buffalo were a town built out of birthday cakes and the whole world showed up to make a wish. People cried the light was so lovely. And all that beauty was made possible because George Westinghouse of Buffalo harnessed Niagara Falls into his alternating current, the same current that would soon be used to fry Leon Czolgosz in the electric chair.

Edison filmed a reenactment of the Czolgosz execution too, but then he would. As Westinghouse's alternating current became more popular than Edison's direct current, Edison launched a smear campaign against Westinghouse in which, attempting to prove the danger of AC, he staged demonstrations electrocuting horses and dogs that caught the eye of New York prison reformers looking for humane methods to carry out capital punishment. Hence the electric chair, first used at the state prison in Auburn in 1890, where Czolgosz would sit in "Old Sparky" eleven years later. Before the verb "to electrocute" came to define death by electricity,

Edison advocated that the verb be named for his nemesis, that a person who had been electrocuted would have been westinghoused instead. I bet Westinghouse came up with some possible definitions of what it meant to be edisoned himself.

Edwin S. Porter, the cinematographer of the Pan-American Exposition, was the Edison Company's film director. Before going on to direct the cinematic landmark *The Great Train Robbery* in 1903, Porter filmed a reenactment of the execution of Leon Czolgosz at New York's Auburn Prison. The company was denied access to film the actual electrocution by Auburn's warden, a man who was so concerned that Czolgosz might turn into a martyred object of outlaw romance that he ordered acid poured on the assassin's corpse so that no one would be tempted to steal then venerate the dead man's clothes or bones.

Porter's film starts with a pan of the exterior of the actual prison and then cuts to the indoors reenactment, in which an actor playing Czolgosz stands behind bars as guards arrive, escorting him to the chair. They strap in his hands, legs and hands, fussing and primping as if they were tailors measuring for a suit. The men clear to the sides of the frame and then Czolgosz's body levitates slightly three times. At the end of the film everyone stands around, staring at the still-seated corpse. It's shocking how matter-of-fact it is. But then the facts of every stage of Leon Czolgosz's life are all like this—brutal but banal.

Czolgosz's childhood involving a wicked stepmother and grimy toil is a Cinderella story, except that at the climax this Cinderella doesn't so much marry the prince as shoot him in

the stomach. One of eight children born to Czech immigrants in Michigan, Czolgosz had to quit school and go to
work in a glass factory for ten or twelve hours a day the year
his mother died. He was twelve. His father remarried a
woman whom Czolgosz despised so much he started skip-
ping meals to avoid her, preferring to drink milk alone in his
room. Like a lot of their fellow Slavs, the family moved
around the Rust Belt of Ohio and Pennsylvania in search of
work. Leon worked ten- or twelve-hour shifts making steel
wires in another hot factory—that's where he got his scar—
until the depression of 1893, when wages were lowered and
he went on strike. Fired, then blacklisted, he got his old job
back by working under the alias Fred Nieman. German for
"nobody," Nieman is the name Czolgosz first gave to the Buffalo police upon arrest.

When Americans first heard of Czolgosz (pronounced
"shol-gosh"), they found comfort in his z-ridden name, relieved that the president of the United States had been assassinated by a foreigner. But Czolgosz was born here. He
was as American as that other son of Slavic Rust Belt immigrants, Pennsylvania's Andrew Warhola, a.k.a. Andy Warhol.

Even Stephen Sondheim cannot tart up Leon Czolgosz.
Czolgosz is such a sad pathetic figure, and by pathetic I mean
drowning in pathos, that he is the one psycho killer in the
musical *Assassins* who never gets a laugh. He is as drab and
morose as Charles Guiteau is snappy. "A scruffy sullen la-
borer" is how the *Assassins* stage directions describe him, as
opposed to Guiteau, who is "seedy but dapper." In one of the
big production numbers, "Gun Song," in which the assassins
gather to extol the history-making virtues of squeezing a trigger, Czolgosz's lyrics are about all the workers who die in the

manufacturing process before a gun is even fired—iron miners, steel mill and factory workers, machinists. "A gun claims many men before it's done," he wails. In terms of musical showstoppers, "Gun Song" is not exactly "Seventy-six Trombones." Come to think of it, Czolgosz would probably know all the ways musical instrument production could maim a guy too.

Having a hard life doesn't justify murder. Insanity might explain it. The travesty of Czolgosz's trial, which lasted eight measly hours, sheds little light on his psychiatric state. Though it's amazing that Czolgosz lived to stand trial at all. In the melee after the shooting, the mob beat him up, crying, "Lynch him!" It was McKinley who actually saved his life. Looking up from his wound to see the assassin getting clobbered, the president commanded, "Go easy on him, boys."

Before his execution, Czolgosz explained, "I killed the president because he was the enemy of the good people—the good working people." Truth was, Czolgosz hadn't held down a job in years. In 1897, the first year of the McKinley administration, Czolgosz suffered some sort of mysterious breakdown, quit working, and started to study socialism and then anarchism, attending meetings in Cleveland and elsewhere. It was in that city that Czolgosz heard the anarchist Emma Goldman speak on May 5, 1901. "She set me on fire," he later told his jailers. This is what he heard her say:

Under the galling yoke of government, ecclesiasticism and the bonds of custom and prejudice it is impossible for the individual to work out his own career as he could wish. Anarchism aims at a new and complete freedom. . . . We merely desire complete individual liberty and this can never be obtained as long as there is an existing government.

After the assassination, forgetting her own descriptions of "the galling yoke of government," Goldman would wonder why Czolgosz chose to attack McKinley instead of "some more direct representative of the system of economic oppression and misery." Surely Goldman was thinking of her ex-boyfriend Alexander Berkman, incarcerated for attempting to murder Henry Frick of the Carnegie Steel Company after Frick had ordered Pinkerton gunmen to open fire on striking workers in Pennsylvania in 1892.

If one applies Goldman's logic to search for an alternative target, a "more direct representative of the system of economic oppression and misery" than McKinley, Robert Todd Lincoln immediately springs to mind. Lincoln had returned to Chicago and his lucrative private law practice after his service in the Garfield and Arthur administrations. George Pullman, founder of the Pullman Palace Car Company, was his most important client. In 1894, Pullman workers were either laid off or had their wages cut. And even though they lived in the company town of Pullman in housing owned by George Pullman, he refused to lower his workers' rents. The resulting Pullman strike became a red-letter date in labor history, bringing socialist Eugene Debs to national attention. Pullman's drawn-out, stubborn refusal to budge on worker demands prompted even "Dollar Mark" Hanna to complain, "A man who won't meet his men half-way is a God-damn fool." Robert Todd Lincoln was Pullman's special counsel through the entire episode. Lincoln's representation of Pullman is consistent with his preference for capital over labor. Take, for example, the Haymarket Riot of 1886, in which a bomb got thrown and anarchist workers employed by the McCormick Reaper Works were hanged as scapegoats. (Their execution, by the way, inspired Emma Goldman to join the anarchist ranks.) In 1893, when Illinois's governor John P. Altgeld committed political suicide to bravely pardon three of the innocent Haymarket defendants who were still rotting in prison, Robert Todd Lincoln, who had vacationed with the McCormick family, gave a speech at Harvard calling Governor Altgeld's mercy a "slander upon justice I must denounce." In 1901, at the time of the McKinley assassination, Robert Todd Lincoln had just become president of the Pullman Company, a position he would hold until 1911. So by Emma Goldman's criteria Robert Todd Lincoln would have made an exceedingly perfect mark for Leon Czolgosz in Buffalo instead of President McKinley. And given his second career as the presidential angel of death, Robert Lincoln was even in town at the time.

After Emma Goldman's Cleveland speech set Leon Czolgosz on fire, he followed her to Chicago, tracking her down at the home of the editor of the anarchist paper *Free Society* at the moment she was rushing off to catch a train. (Sondheim and his collaborator John Weidman scripted this brief meeting as a love scene in *Assassins*.) He introduced himself as Nieman, then stuck around after she left to quiz her editor friend whether they were having any "secret meetings." The editor, thinking Nieman was a narc, printed a warning against him in *Free Society*, calling him a possible spy the anarchist community should look out for, claiming that he pretended "to be greatly interested in the cause, asking for names, or soliciting aid for acts of contemplated violence."

Goldman was appalled by the ad. She complained, had the smear retracted, but too late. Czolgosz was already in Buffalo, about to prove what a true anarchist he was.

Years later, in her riveting autobiography *Living My Life*, Goldman, recalling the fervor with which Nieman/Czolgosz had asked her to recommend books he should read, wrote that "it must have hurt him to the quick to be so cruelly misjudged by the very people to whom he had come for inspiration."

Emma Goldman claimed to abhor violence, and yet her speeches and writings are full of sympathetic odes to killers and would-be killers, Czolgosz included. I'm more of a Ten Commandments, rule-of-law girl myself. The closest I've ever come to anarchy is buying a Sex Pistols record. I find Goldman fascinating, but bothersome. (Especially her blasé recounting of being Berkman's accomplice in shooting Frick.) While her apologies for violence were loathsome and her utopian hooey about life without government childish, her book's description of making friends with her fellow anarchists in New York is enchanting. Which is why her guilty assumption that Czolgosz would have been hurt by the anarchist paper's warning—page 309 in my copy—is so poignant. The three hundred preceding pages are crammed with anecdotes and evidence of her entanglements and camaraderie. In fact, when I read her remarkable account of her first week in New York, when she met Berkman, who would become her lover, and Johann Most, who would become her mentor, I wanted to retrace her steps.

So one night, after a movie, my friend Bennett and I walked down Orchard Street to Canal to see where Emma's aunt and uncle's apartment used to be. It was her first stop in New York. I fill in Bennett about her giddy introduction to the city and then we reminisced about our own arrivals. He tells a funny story about being a college freshman and going to Times Square, where he was offered a new drug called crack. I recount the bohemian romance of how I lucked into a sublet thanks to the financial columnist at *Esquire*.

"Perhaps," as Truman Capote once confessed as he exaggerated his Brooklyn neighborhood's charms, "I take too Valentine a view." But I've been lucky enough to go on swell walks with talkative people all over the world, and there really is something speedier and hopped up and deep about the magnificently blabbermouth nature of friendship in New York, and Goldman's book is further proof of this.

Goldman's description of her beginning here is a charming blur. She meets the most important people in her life, all the while eating and talking and walking around, drunk on ideas, friendship, and lust—and wine, her first. For example, in one breathtaking paragraph she is (I think) losing her virginity to Berkman (she had been married but to an impotent husband); meanwhile, what's going through her head is the question, "Can idealists be cruel?" It's thrilling, even though I did want to reach into the page and pat her head, breaking it to her that, Oh my dear, idealists are the cruelest monsters of them all.

The meetings she describes, the dinners, the walks in the parks with hotheads who speak in manifestos—that's what Czolgosz craved. There is an aching loneliness in his denials to the police that Emma Goldman helped him shoot the president. "I had no confidants," he insisted, "no one to help me. I was alone absolutely."

Nevertheless, Goldman was jailed under suspicion of

being Czolgosz's accomplice. Though Goldman was eventually released if not exactly cleared, she became a pariah, receiving hate mail such as, "You damn bitch of an anarchist. I wish I could get at you. I would tear your heart out and feed it to my dog."

As Theodore Roosevelt, the new president, would put it in his first message to Congress, "The American people are slow to wrath, but when their wrath is once kindled it burns like a consuming flame." Roosevelt, his wrath lit up like a wad of newspaper soaked in moonshine, continued:

> For the anarchist himself, whether he preaches or practices his doctrines, we need not have one particle more concern than for any ordinary murderer. He is not the victim of social or political injustice. There are no wrongs to remedy in his case. The cause of his criminality is to be found in his own evil passions and in the evil conduct of those who urge him on, not in any failure by others or by the State to do justice to him or his. He is a malefactor and nothing else. He is in no sense, in no shape or way, a "product of social conditions," save as a highwayman is "produced" by the fact than an unarmed man happens to have a purse. . . . Anarchistic speeches, writings, and meetings are essentially seditious and treasonable.

Then he called for legislation barring these talkative traitors from emigrating to the United States. Congress passed the Anarchist Exclusion Act in 1903. It was the first law allowing potential immigrants to be questioned about their political views.

On my walk home from that Canal Street jaunt reliving

Emma's first delirious week in New York, I swung by one of her old apartments on East Thirteenth Street. I read somewhere that her place now rents for four thousand dollars a month. There's an Emma Goldman plaque on the side of the building calling her an "anarchist, orator and advocate of free speech and free love." It concludes, "She was deported to the Soviet Union in 1919." She and Berkman were kicked out of the country for speaking out against the United States' entry into World War I, or as she put it, "for having an opinion."

Walking westward, I passed by the Brevoort Apartments on Fifth Avenue, the site of an old watering hole where Goldman and Berkman had one of their farewell dinners with old friends before being exiled to Russia. "One does not live in a country thirty-four years and find it easy to go," she bemoaned. "All the turmoil of body and soul, all the love and hate that come to an intense human being have come to me here."

It was a warm spring night, but I shivered, feeling lucky to go home.

The Anarchist Exclusion Act strikes me as reactionary. I do believe that anyone coming here has the right to *say* whatever they want, however foolish, insane, or mean. Though Theodore Roosevelt cracked down on people like Emma Goldman, he did okay by people like Leon Czolgosz's people—the workers, the miners, the poor. Calling his agenda the "square deal," he achieved an unprecedented happy medium between the demands of labor and capital, settling a coal strike in 1902 in which he forced the owners to raise wages and stick to a maximum nine-hour workday, but prevented the workers from forming a union. (Nobody was entirely happy, but compared to the bloody strikes of the 1890s, it was an innovation in that nobody got killed.) Roosevelt also coined the term "muckrakers" to describe the crusading journalists like Ida Tarbell, who had taken on the monolith of Standard Oil, and Upton Sinclair, whose book *The Jungle* detailed the horrors of the meatpacking industry. Roosevelt acted on the abuses they brought to light, pursuing dozens of antitrust suits and signing into law the Pure Food and Drug Act of 1906.

I think Roosevelt's soft spot for the underdog in Washington was the influence of New York City—his aristocratic upbringing here and its resultant noblesse oblige. Unlike the ruthless nouveau riches like Standard Oil's self-made John D. Rockefeller, Roosevelt had the easygoing morals of someone who was born rich. But also, back during his days as police commissioner in Manhattan, Roosevelt used to tramp around at night in the company of photographer and reporter Jacob Riis. If you want a clear picture of the gulf between the rich and the poor of Roosevelt's era, go to the Museum of the City of New York, where you can look at a Riis photograph of a cobbler on Ludlow Street sitting down to a Sabbath dinner in the filthy coal cellar he calls home, and then take the elevator up to the installations of rooms from Rockefeller's house, with his stupid solid gold fireplace poker and the cartoonish safe he kept right next to his bed.

The way Riis remembered making Roosevelt's acquaintance in the first place is a likable anecdote. After reading Riis's 1890 book *How the Other Half Lives*, about the poverty and squalor endured by immigrants on the Lower East Side, Roosevelt sent Riis a note that simply said, "How can I help?"

"I was still ignorant of the extent to which big men of great wealth played a mischievous part in our industrial and social life," Roosevelt later wrote in his autobiography about the effect of reading and meeting Riis. "But I was well awake to the need of making ours in good faith both an economic and an industrial as well as a political democracy." Of course, Roosevelt published that in 1913. And he wasn't a Republican anymore.

*

I phoned my friend Matt. "Remember last summer when you asked me to go hiking in the Adirondacks and I told you that one of the reasons I moved away from Montana was so that I wouldn't get asked to do outdoorsy stuff like that anymore?" I asked.

"Yes."

"Well, do you still want to go hiking in the damn Adirondacks? Have you heard of something called Mount Marcy?"

He does and he has. Marcy is the highest peak in the range. Luckily, Matt's goal to climb every peak in the Adirondacks overlaps with my goal of McKinley assassination pilgrimage.

As President McKinley lay dying, Vice President Theodore Roosevelt wasn't sitting in some office somewhere when the cabinet summoned him to Buffalo to take the presidential oath. Nope, he was up enjoying a "bully good tramp" at the highest point in the state of New York. And the story of how he got to Buffalo is like a lot of Roosevelt stories—swashbuckling, death-defying, and hard to believe. Even though he is the only president who was born and raised in New York City, that's not how we think of him. Even here, in his hometown memorial at the entrance to the American Museum of Natural History, the statue of Roosevelt rides a horse. Chiseled into the front of the building are all the many words that describe him—"ranchman, scholar, explorer, scientist, conservationist, naturalist, statesman, author, historian, humanitarian, soldier, patriot," all of which add up to the unspoken "better than you."

Matt, an urbanite with the woods in his heart, is the most Theodore Roosevelt–like friend I have. That probably isn't saying much, as I spend most of my free time indoors around people who talk about politics and entertainment, sprinkling conversations about action movies with insights such as "It wasn't subversive the way *Starship Troopers* was subversive" or debating which founding father can be equated with which founding father of rock 'n' roll—Thomas Paine = Chuck Berry, Ben Franklin = the Big Bopper, etc. (Though Bill Haley = Thomas Jefferson? As if.)

Matt lives next door to a police station around the corner from me in Chelsea. I call his apartment "the cabin," an outpost of old-fashioned piney woodsyness nestled behind a forest of cop cars. I quizzed him once about his roughhewn interior decorating, and he wasn't sure why he was drawn to musty quilts and things made out of logs. "Do I just like nineteenth-century America, or is it just a past I can't have? If it were 1901 right now would I be gaga over tricornered hats and you would come into my apartment and tell me, 'This is so colonial'?"

Recently, he bought an actual cabin, a fixer-upper in Maine. A native of the not particularly rustic Quad Cities of Illinois, Matt claims New York City brought out the backwoodsman in him. "Within six months of moving here, I wanted to buy a car and strap a canoe on top."

Even though Matt is the sort of person who will mention his new rated-to-twenty-degrees-below-zero sleeping bag, the call of the wild is simply one of his many callings. He's learning Spanish. He reads. He shops. On our last road trip together, I noticed that he is the sort of guy who will sing along with "Born to Be Wild" on the car radio while driving to an outlet mall from the FDR Presidential Library.

So one Friday night in November, I meet him after he gets off work and we drive toward the Adirondacks. We get as far as a hotel in Lake George. I go to bed early, resting up for the dreaded hike. At breakfast the next morning, I ask him, "What did you do last night?"

"I went to a bar. I ate a burger and drank a beer and read a book about string theory." Just like Roosevelt on his North Dakota ranch, rustling steers by day, reading Poe after dark.

I have already reneged on the Mount Marcy climb. I looked it up and it's a twenty-mile round-trip hike. Nearby Rooster Comb, five miles from the parking lot and back, is more my speed, though daunting nevertheless. Plus, I argue, we can't see the top of Mount Marcy *from* the top of Mount Marcy. The smaller, shorter peak is supposed to have a great view of it, offering perspective on Roosevelt and per-spective is why we're here, right?

When McKinley was attacked, Roosevelt rushed from Lake Champlain to McKinley's bedside in Buffalo. When the president appeared to be on the mend, McKinley's advi-sors shooed Roosevelt out of town, thinking that the vice president's removal sent a message of recovery and hope. So

Roosevelt came to the Adirondacks, joining his wife and children who were already staying at a lodge called the Tahawus Club. When he got there, he was pleased to learn that his son, Theodore Jr., had just bagged his very first deer.

Roosevelt, a guide, and a few other Tahawus guests climbed Mount Marcy on September 13, 1901. It was raining. Today, it's sunny but cold. There are patches of snow here and there up the trail, the very steep trail. There are plenty of switchbacks, and it's beautiful, all forest and boulders and cliffs, but did I mention how steep it is? I love walking. Walking might be my favorite pastime. It's one of the reasons I moved to the pedestrian paradise that is New York City. It's hiking I try to avoid. To pace myself, I decide to pretend I'm walking in Manhattan, asking Matt to measure out the two and a half miles up the mountain that way. "Like, say I'm starting at Fourteenth Street, at Union Square, and I'm walking north. What street is the summit?"

"The top of Times Square? Maybe Broadway and Fifty-fourth?"

So that's what I do to cheer myself on. At the halfway point—those Korean restaurants on Thirty-second—I know I'll make it to the top. When Roosevelt reached the summit of Mount Marcy, he kept exclaiming, "Beautiful country! Beautiful country!" Me, I just wheeze.

"I wore the wrong gear," Matt says. "I made the mistake of not wearing a wicking layer." He looks around at the view, remembering why we're here. "Teddy Roosevelt probably didn't have a wicking layer, and I bet he wasn't complaining."

On Marcy, Roosevelt and his party stopped for a lunch at Lake Tear-in-the-Clouds, then thought to be the source of the Hudson River. Roosevelt happily dug in to a tin of ox tongue. (Matt's mountain climbing reward is an organic cookie.) Roosevelt then spotted a man coming toward him. He later remembered that he "was looking forward to dinner with the interest only an appetite worked up in the woods gives you." And how. I'm staring at one of the grandest views in the Northeast and all I can see is steak. Roosevelt continued, "When I saw the runner I instinctively knew he had bad news—the worst news in the world." He was right. It was a telegram:

THE PRESIDENT IS CRITICALLY ILL
HIS CONDITION IS GRAVE
OXYGEN IS BEING GIVEN
ABSOLUTELY NO HOPE

Roosevelt, much to the dismay of the guy who sprinted uphill for twelve miles to deliver the telegram, sat back down and finished his lunch. After that, finally, he started the climb down from the mountaintop toward the trailhead that was the White House.

At the Tahawus Club, another bossier telegram, along with supper, was waiting for him:

THE PRESIDENT APPEARS TO BE DYING AND
MEMBERS OF THE CABINET IN BUFFALO
THINK YOU SHOULD LOSE NO TIME COMING

The Tahawus Club is still here. It's very well kept, freshly painted yellow. Rocking chairs on the porch rock in the wind. When Roosevelt and his wife, Edith, were staying here, the other guests referred to their deer-slaying children as "the little Indians." One of them, Archibald, remembered that on that 1901 trip he overheard women in the rocking chairs talking about how "Mr. McKinley had been shot in the abdomen. I remember puzzling over this word for quite a while and finally asking what it was. I was much disappointed when I found out that 'abdomen' was nothing but a stomach."

It was almost midnight when Archibald Roosevelt's father climbed into a buggy to ride down the mountain in the dark to the train station at North Creek, thirty-five miles away. Nowadays that road, 28N, is paved. It is named in his honor, the Roosevelt-Marcy Byway. Even with the asphalt, even in the daylight and in a car, it's a tricky drive, narrow and curving, a corridor of trees.

On 28N, near Newcomb, a rock monument erected in 1908 marks the approximate spot where Roosevelt became president at 2:15 A.M. on September 14, 1901, McKinley's time of death. It's kind of shaped like a hug, listing the names of David Hunter, Orrin Kellogg, and Michael Cronin, the brave local relay drivers who were kind and/or demented enough to get the new president to his train.

Around three-thirty that morning, Kellogg dropped off Roosevelt at Aiden Lair, Cronin's hunting lodge. The place still stands, but barely. Once, it must have been inviting and cozy, its tall rock chimney spitting smoke from the fireplace. Now, it sags. It's falling in, falling down. The windows that weren't boarded up are broken. "Looks like we can trespass readily," says Matt, getting out of the car. Around back, there's a lovely little brook, but also a better view into the lodge's ripped-up insides—glass shards poking out everywhere, insulation oozing out of the ceiling, a crusty old pair of underwear wadded up next to a rusty beer can on top of what used to be the floor.

When Roosevelt arrived, Mike Cronin knew McKinley was already dead, but he kept the news from Roosevelt, thinking the trip itself was going to be worrisome enough. "It was the darkest night I ever saw," Cronin remembered later, adding, "Mr. Roosevelt was one of the nerviest men I ever saw and I am not easily scared myself. At one place, while we were going down a slippery hill, one of the horses stumbled. It was a ticklish bit of road and I was beginning to get somewhat uneasy and began holding the team back, but Mr. Roosevelt said, 'Oh, that doesn't matter. Push ahead!' "

Driving down that road, Matt says, "I guess they must have had lanterns at the front of the buggy."

"They had one lantern," I say, "and Roosevelt was holding it."

"How terrifying this must have looked at three A.M.," Matt says, passing a sign that warns ROUGH ROAD.

At dawn, Cronin's horses Frank and Dick clickety-clomped into North Creek. Roosevelt's secretary was waiting for him at the train station, handing him another telegram from Secretary of State John Hay. "The president died at two-fifteen this morning," it said.

That depot, a cute wooden building built in 1875, was once the northern terminus of the Adirondack railroad. It's now a museum in Roosevelt's honor, his "night ride to the presidency" being the biggest thing that ever happened around here. The museum is closed when Matt and I arrive, but there's a whole exhibit about Roosevelt outside—a kiosk of photos (Cronin with Frank and Dick, Roosevelt at various ages) and text (the telegrams about McKinley, an endorsement from Governor Pataki, a believable quote in which Roosevelt brags, "No man has had a happier life than I have had, a happier life in every way").

"There's something Olympian about him," Matt says. "Or Paul Revere. He's Paul Revere riding down Mount Olympus, climbing the mountain by day, holding the lantern on a buggy on his way to becoming president and running the United States. That is a singular definition of power."

The September 22, 1901, edition of the *New York Herald* headlined its Roosevelt-in-the-Adirondacks article thus: "That Wild Ride Down the Mountain Side. Leading a Charge of Troopers at San Juan Less Hazardous Than Spinning Through Darkness Along the Edge of Great Precipices."

A couple of weeks earlier, when Roosevelt first heard the news that McKinley had been attacked, the then–vice president said of the assassin, "If it had been I, he wouldn't have gotten away so easily. I think I'd have guzzled him."

He's probably right. In 1912, when Roosevelt was in Milwaukee campaigning as the Bull Moose presidential candidate, would-be assassin John Schrank shot him at close range with a .38. Schrank claimed the ghost of William McKinley came to him in a dream and said of Roosevelt, "This is my murderer. Avenge my death." The bullet was slowed down by the contents of Roosevelt's chest pocket, a steel eyeglass case and the thick, folded text of the speech he was about to give. (The dinged case is on display at the Roosevelt birthplace in New York; the dinted papers in the Smithsonian.) Though bleeding, Roosevelt delivered his speech, pulling the bloodstained papers out of his pocket, crowing, "You see, it takes more than one bullet to kill a Bull Moose."

Though the Roosevelt presidency had already begun Roosevelt-style in the mountains with the noisy racket of hoofbeats in the dark, Buffalo was muffled by McKinley's death. Getting off the train, Roosevelt went straight to his friend Ansley Wilcox's mansion, borrowed a proper coat, paid his respects to Mrs. McKinley, and then returned to Wilcox's house to be sworn in. The house, with a pediment and columned porch, looks Greek enough to substitute for the usual ceremony amidst the columns of the U.S. Capitol. It's now a museum administered by the National Park Service, the Theodore Roosevelt Inaugural National Historic Site.

Roosevelt took the oath here in the library on the first floor, a warm, brown Victorian room with a fireplace and leather chairs. The Park Service has a video playing, a reenactment of the ceremony produced for its centennial. It's quite effective, capturing the mournful silence of that moment. There are times when the loudest thing happening is the light shining through the windows. More than fifty people, including future president Woodrow Wilson, crowded in here to watch, reporters included (though they were forbidden to take photographs).

According to the following day's *Buffalo Courier*, when Secretary of War Elihu Root started to administer the oath, he broke down weeping "and for fully a minute he could not utter another word," which made everyone else bow their heads and tear up too. "The Vice-President's eyes were moist and he clutched nervously at the lapel of his frock coat."

"I shall take the oath at once in accord with the request

of you members of the Cabinet," Roosevelt said. He continued,

> In this hour of our deep and terrible bereavement I wish to state that it shall be my aim to continue absolutely unbroken the policy of President McKinley for the peace, the prosperity and the honor of our beloved country.

The house displays the desk where Roosevelt wrote those words. It also features an exhibit of relics associated with Roosevelt and McKinley—the serpentine walking stick Roosevelt hiked Mount Marcy with, a Pan-Am commemorative plate decorated with the seal of North and South America holding hands, and, talk about sentimental, the "telegraph wires that were used to carry notice of McKinley's death to local newspapers."

The aforementioned nervously clutched black frock coat Roosevelt had borrowed for the swearing-in is also on display. Seeing the clothes in which Roosevelt became president reminds me of a letter Roosevelt soon received from Robert Todd Lincoln. Roosevelt had bumped into Lincoln here in Buffalo before heading to the Adirondacks. Lincoln had brought his family to town to see the Pan-American Exposition, never suspecting their vacation would see him reprise his cameo role as presidential assassination omen for the third and final time. Lincoln wrote to the new president, "I do not congratulate you for I have seen too much of the seamy side of the Presidential Robe to think of it as a desirable garment, but I do hope that you will have the strength and courage to carry you through a successful administration." Roosevelt must have wanted to write back to Robert

Todd—*tod*, the German word for death—Lincoln, "Well, since you brought it up, can I interest you in a diplomatic appointment in Katmandu?"

In downtown Buffalo, there's a memorial to McKinley, an obelisk guarded by marble lions—the sorry-you-got-shafted shaft. My nephew Owen loved the lions so much he threw a weepy temper tantrum when we tried to leave. As my sister and I pried him off a marble paw he kicked us, screaming, "I want lions!" Coming between kids and their presidential monuments is like getting caught between a lioness and her cubs.

McKinley lay in state in downtown Buffalo before Roosevelt escorted his coffin back to Washington. Thousands stood in line in the rain to pay their respects, including James Parker, the black waiter who was standing in the receiving line at the Temple of Music and clocked Leon Czolgosz.

In one ultimate Pan-American moment, Geronimo himself strutted past the coffin. One of the Indians riding in the faux battles staged at the exposition, the sexagenarian Apache warrior who fought the Mexicans as a young man and then the Americans after they defeated the Mexicans was still technically a U.S. prisoner of war in the custody of armed guards. He enclosed a card with a memorial wreath for McKinley. He wrote, "The rainbow of hope is out of the sky. Heavy clouds hang about us. Tears wet the ground of the tepees. The chief of the nation is dead. Farewell." Geronimo had probably buried so many people by then he could knock out a eulogy in his sleep. Four years later, he would ride in Roosevelt's inaugural parade, cornering TR after the festivities and begging to be allowed to go back home to what was now New Mexico to die where he was born, pleading, "Great

Father, my hands are tied as with a rope. . . . I pray you to cut the ropes and make me free. Let me die in my own country, as an old man who has been punished enough and is free." To no avail—he passed away in 1909 in Oklahoma, incarcerated at Fort Still.

Unfortunately for Roosevelt, the McKinley assassination had a theme song. Reportedly among the dying president's last words was the title of his favorite hymn, "Nearer My God to Thee." So a quartet sang the song in the Milburn house before the body was ushered out, where a band across the street repeated it as the coffin was carried out the door. As Roosevelt accompanied his predecessor's coffin from Buffalo to Washington and on to Canton for burial, mourners serenaded the train. At Harrisburg, for instance, thousands bellowed "Nearer My God to Thee" from the platform of the station. Then they played it at the White House, then again at the Capitol rotunda. Roosevelt must have groaned every time he heard the lines "Still all my songs shall be, nearer my God to thee."

Soon enough, though, Roosevelt would be singing his own theme song, which I like to think of as an arrangement of the Kinks' "I'm Not Like Everybody Else" butchered by a high school marching band. Roosevelt took the melody he helped McKinley compose, the idea that the United States was poised for global domination, and then he went electric. Roosevelt built the Panama Canal, earned a Nobel Prize brokering a peace treaty between Russia and Japan, secured Moroccan independence, and sent the "Great White Fleet" of the U.S. Navy on tour around the globe to warn the world that the United States was a power to contend with.

When McKinley was attacked, Roosevelt complained that

he didn't want to get to the presidency "through the grave-yard." In 1904, the American people elected Roosevelt in his own right. To make up for the solemn silence of his first swearing-in, his second was a wingding of parties and parades. And on March 4, 1905, when Roosevelt took the oath of office for the second time, he wore a ring given to him by Secretary of State John Hay. The ring contained the hair of Abraham Lincoln.

Scenes from the life of Robert Todd Lincoln, a.k.a. Jinxy McDeath. Abraham Lincoln's eldest son had the misfortune of attending his father's deathbed after his assassination in 1865, witnessing the assassination of James A. Garfield in Washington in 1881, and detraining in Buffalo in 1901 to learn that William McKinley had been assassinated mere moments before his arrival. Robert Lincoln lived a long life, attending the Lincoln Memorial dedication ceremony in 1922.

CHAPTER FOUR

The America that Lincoln was bred in, the homespun and humane and humorous America that he wished to preserve, has nothing in common with the sedulously classic monument that was erected to his memory. Who lives in that shrine, I wonder—Lincoln, or the men who conceived it: the leader who beheld the mournful victory of the Civil War, or the generation that took pleasure in the mean triumph of the Spanish-American exploit, and placed the imperial standard in the Philippines and the Caribbean?

LEWIS MUMFORD *Sticks and Stones: A Study of American Architecture and Civilization, 1924*

In 1904, Theodore Roosevelt's secretary of war, William Howard Taft, sent his fellow Republican, architect Daniel Burnham, to the Philippines (where Taft had recently served as the new U.S. territory's governor). Burnham's assignment was to draw a new plan for the city of Manila. Burnham had been the mastermind behind the 1893 World's Columbian Exposition in Chicago. That fair was an architectural watershed. The "White City," a neoclassical enclave on the shores of Lake Michigan, would spark what came to be known as the City Beautiful movement of urban design, involving

Greco-Roman buildings and monuments erected on geometric street grids among grand boulevards and restful, pretty parks. After the success of the fair, Chicago businessmen hired Burnham to draw up new plans for the lakefront and eventually the city as a whole. Before he did, like so many artists and architects of his generation, Burnham took off on a European study trip, where he got religion—pagan religion. Always drawn to classicism, Burnham described Rome as a "delight." His travels in Greece, and especially staring at the Athens Acropolis crowned with the Parthenon, converted him from a Sunday classicist to an evangelist of columns and pediments. "I have," he claimed, "the spirit of Greece once and forever stamped on my soul."

At the same time Burnham was trying to turn the Philippine capital into Chicago—and Manila could do a lot worse —Burnham was making his mark on our nation's capital by serving on the 1901–02 McMillan Senate Park Commission for the Improvement of Washington, D.C. If you have gone sightseeing in Washington, you have walked around inside Burnham's head.

Burnham and his fellow commissioners hoped to turn the Mall into "a work of civic art." They decided to carry out Pierre L'Enfant's original plan for the Mall as an unobstructed open space, which required tearing down the Baltimore & Potomac Railroad station where President Garfield got shot. (They replaced it with the present-day depot a few blocks away, Union Station, designed by Burnham.) Also, the commission ratified the digging of the Reflecting Pool, the construction of a bridge to Arlington Cemetery, and the radical notion of erecting a memorial to Abraham Lincoln on the drained swamp next to the river.

The McMillan Commission begat the 1902 Lincoln Memorial Commission starring Secretary of State and former Lincoln secretary John Hay. Pleased that the shrine honoring his late boss would go up in what was then a remote location, Hay remarked that Lincoln "was of the immortals. You must not approach too close to the immortals. His monument should stand alone . . . isolated, distinguished, and serene."

In 1910, William Howard Taft, now president, established the United States Commission of Fine Arts—Washington loves a commission—to advise the government on aesthetic matters having to do with art, architecture, planning, and design. (It still does.) Taft appointed men to his commission who were boosters of the previous commissions, including architects Burnham and Cass Gilbert and sculptor Daniel Chester French, whose cronies would soon offer him the gig of sculpting Lincoln.

Three years earlier, Gilbert and French had collaborated on the new neoclassical New York Custom House near the docks downtown. It was built to replace the old stomping grounds of Chester Arthur and Herman Melville. If trade and the money that comes with it were cash cows during the administrations of Hayes and Garfield, the influx of goods from America's new colonial ports in the Caribbean, as well as the anticipated booty from the Panama Canal, the new improved Custom House symbolized the emerging economic global dominance of Theodore Roosevelt's America. French was assigned to sculpt allegorical figures of the continents. His *America,* from 1907, is one of the most concise depictions of our history I've ever seen: a European stepping on a Mayan head. (Ironically, after U.S. Customs decamped to offices in the World Trade Center in 1973, Gilbert's building became the National Museum of the American Indian. Thus does a sculpture about native subjugation guard the door to a place devoted to preserving and celebrating Native American culture.)

One afternoon, I walked downtown from my apartment in Chelsea to look at Gilbert's design and French's sculptures. When I was researching the people and places having some connection to the McKinley administration, I came across the names of architects and artists Burnham, Gilbert, and French about nine thousand times. But I never studied them in school, and I have a master's degree in art history. Standing downtown looking at French's 1907 *America* step on the Mayan mask next to his similarly questionable *Africa* reminded me of what I had been taught about the art and architecture of the period—Pablo Picasso and Frank Lloyd Wright.

Picasso was of the generation of young Spaniards who made their mark after the war they called "*el Desastre del 98,*" the disaster in which the United States won the remnants of the Spanish empire, known here as the Spanish-American War. In 1907, the same year French sculpted *America,* Picasso made one of the most influential paintings of the twentieth century, *Les Demoiselles d'Avignon.* Back in school, I took essay exams and wrote papers about this painting all the time. And one thing the A student is supposed to say about it is that three of the five nude prostitutes in the picture have the faces of African masks. Picasso saw the beauty in African art, just as Frank Lloyd Wright saw the beauty in Mayan architecture. To Wright, the Mayans weren't a people to step

ASSASSINATION VACATION

on, they were a people to learn from, a people with ideas worth stealing. (If you want to get a clear picture of this turn-of-the-twentieth-century aesthetic and moral clash, go to Buffalo, where you can leave the Burnham-inspired neoclassical white columns of the Buffalo and Erie County Historical Society Museum, built for the Pan-American Exposition of 1901, and walk basically around the corner to see the earthy horizontals of Frank Lloyd Wright's prairie-style Darwin Martin house built in 1903. Those two years between the buildings might as well be two centuries they look so different. One is ancient history, the other sci-fi.)

There are two reasons I find this classicism versus modernism tiff interesting to think about. First, from this side of the twentieth century, après strip malls, fast-food franchises, glass boxes, housing projects, and other architectural gaffes, it's fun to look back on this dilemma of to-column-or-not-to-column, because honestly, the only question most Americans ask about a new building at this point is basically: Is it a soul-sucking eyesore of cheap-ass despair? It's not? Whew.

Secondly, with a building as iconic as the Lincoln Memorial, it's such a given, seems so inevitable, I cannot imagine the Mall without it. Moreover, it's so universally revered it's hard to believe there were ever protests against the way it looked. But when Daniel Burnham, Cass Gilbert, Daniel Chester French, and their fellow commissioners chose Henry Bacon's Greek temple design for the Lincoln Memorial in 1913, the Chicago chapter of the American Institute of Architects, led by an associate of Frank Lloyd Wright's, threw a fit. Understandably, the prairie school architects from the Land

243

of Lincoln were outraged that the Lincoln Memorial was going to be so "purely Greek and entirely un-American."

Henry Bacon's previous buildings included a Greek-looking bank still standing on New York's Union Square and the Greek-looking tomb for Republican boss Mark Hanna in Cleveland's Lakeview Cemetery. Bacon and French had already collaborated on a tomb for Chicago retail magnate Marshall Field. So by the time they were hired to work on the Lincoln Memorial, they were the Republican Party's top marble go-to guys.

It's amusing to speculate on what kind of low, flat slab Frank Lloyd Wright might have come up with to honor the tall, skinny Lincoln. It's more intriguing still to imagine what Wright's Chicago mentor Louis Sullivan might have designed had he been asked. Sullivan is my favorite architect for the same reason Lincoln is my favorite president—his buildings are logical but warm, pragmatic but not without frippery, grand and human all at once. It's telling that when Daniel Burnham got back from Europe he started drawing Doric columns, and when Louis Sullivan returned to Chicago from his European study sojourn he started taking long walks out on the prairie. Sullivan accused the classical influence of Burnham's World's Fair of being a "virus," a "violent outbreak" of the "bogus antique." Whereas Burnham's aesthetic, shared by Henry Bacon, attempted to catapult Abraham Lincoln up to Mount Olympus—"isolated, distinguished, and serene" just like John Hay hoped—Sullivan's buildings live here on earth. Having strode so often on the prairie that Lincoln also walked upon, Sullivan thought stalks of wheat were as inspiring as the columns of the Parthenon and hoped that his fellow Americans could build their own new country out of the one Lincoln had saved. Sullivan complained in his 1924 autobiography about the sort-of-Greek, kind-of-Roman buildings springing up all over the United States, including the recently dedicated Lincoln Memorial, that

> In a land declaring its fervid democracy, its inventiveness, its resourcefulness, its unique daring, enterprise and progress thus did the virus of a culture, snobbish and alien to the land, perform its work of disintegration; and thus ever works the pallid academic mind, denying the real, exalting the fictitious and the false, incapable of adjusting itself to the flow of living things, to the reality and the pathos of man's follies, to the valiant hope that ever causes him to aspire, and again to aspire; that never lifts a hand in aid because it cannot . . . when what the world needs is courage, common sense and human sympathy, and a moral standard that is plain, valid and livable.

What I wouldn't give to see what a man like that would have conjured in honor of a man like Lincoln. What if this memorial, and, while we're at it, all three branches of government, were more courageous and sympathetic and made more sense and aspired and again aspired? What if the pallid and the academic, the fictitious and the false were banished from this Mall and from this town? Spend too much time pondering what-ifs like that about the nation's capital and you'll want to hurl yourself off the Washington Monument.

Thanks to congressional feet-dragging, political infighting, World War I, and the simple time-consuming process of mining then shipping tons upon tons of marble all the way

from Colorado, by the time the Lincoln Memorial was dedicated in 1922, Abraham Lincoln had been dead for fifty-
seven years. There is a wonderful photograph of a clearly
enchanted Robert Todd Lincoln sitting in the audience at
the ceremony—sitting with the white people in the audience. Because the Lincoln Memorial dedication ceremony
was segregated. Segregated!

So it took a while for the Lincoln Memorial to come to
mean what it's come to mean. Thanks to Marian Anderson,
who performed here on Easter Sunday 1939 after the Daughters of the American Revolution barred her from singing at
Constitution Hall because of her skin color and of course
Martin Luther King Jr., who stood on what he called "this
hallowed spot" in 1963 making history with "I have a dream,"
the memorial has long been physically and philosophically
desegregated.

So much so in fact that one time I came to the memorial
with my friend Dave and as we were climbing the steps he
said, "It looks fake."

"What does?"

"These people," he said, pointing at the other visitors.
"Look at them. Every color, from all over the world."

"Why is that fake?"

"It's too perfect, like they were brought here by a casting
agent to make a commercial."

He was right. The people who visit the memorial always
look like an advertisement for democracy, so bizarrely, suspiciously diverse that one time I actually saw a man in a cowboy
hat standing there reading the Gettysburg Address next to a
Hasidic Jew. I wouldn't have been surprised if they had
linked arms with a woman in a burka and a Masai warrior, to

belt out "It's a Small World After All" flanked by a chorus line of nuns and field-tripping, rainbow-skinned schoolchildren.

Yes, the memorial is lousy with coldhearted columns, a white Greek temple for a man associated with browns and blacks—the log cabin, the prairie, the top hat, the skin of slaves. Yes, Lewis Mumford called it a memorial to the Spanish-American War and he's not all wrong. But loving this memorial is a lot like loving this country: I might not have built the place this way; it's a little too pompous, and if you look underneath the marble, the structure's a fake and ye olde Parthenon is actually supported by skyscraper steel. But the Lincoln Memorial is still my favorite place in the world and not just in spite of its many stupid flaws. It's my favorite place partly because of its blankness, because of those columns that are such standard-issue Western civ clichés they don't so much exist as float. Inside the Lincoln Memorial I know what Frederick Douglass meant when he described what it was like to be invited to Lincoln's White House: "I felt big there."

Never underestimate the corrective lens that is sentimentality. Take, for example, the new National World War II Memorial next to the Washington Monument. Each state gets its own bland stone pillar. The first time I see it I hate it at once, think it mucks up the Mall, but nevertheless search for the granite Oklahoma pylon because my late uncle, John A. Parson, served in the Philippines. Damndest thing, but the instant I spot it, "Oklahoma," I burst into tears. One time I asked him about his service and he told me about fighting the Japanese for control of a hill. It took a month and it was raining the whole time. He said they only gained a couple of inches every day, every day in the rain. His socks, he said, were never dry. A month to get up a hill while being shot at in wet socks. John A. died a couple of years ago. Suddenly and forever the World War II Memorial stopped being clunky architecture and turned into the sound of my uncle's voice telling me that story. Now I don't care what it looks like. They could have carved it out of chewed bubble gum and I would think of it fondly.

*

On the Saturday before Easter, there is an empty bandstand set up at the bottom of the Lincoln Memorial's steps. I ask a National Park Service ranger what it's for. He replies that a church from suburban Virginia is hosting an Easter sunrise service here in the morning.

I snap, "How did *they* get permission to do that?"

He shrugs, nonchalantly answering, "They applied for a permit."

Then I remembered that a couple of weeks from now there is an abortion rights rally scheduled to take place here on the Mall, that the pro-choice people probably applied for the exact same permit. I like that. I like that the Mall serves as our national Tupperware, reliable and empty, waiting to be filled with potluck whatever.

Besides, an Easter service at the Lincoln Memorial does make historical sense. Booth shot Lincoln on Good Friday, the day commemorating Christ's crucifixion. By the next morning, Lincoln was dead. How stupid was Booth? What kind of moron does away with the president he hates at the kickoff of Easter weekend? Sunday morning, pulpits across the land shouted analogies comparing the martyred president to the martyred Christ. Richard Eddy, pastor of the

First Universalist Church of Philadelphia, asked his congregation, "Was there ever since the death of the savior of the world, a more brutal, a more uncalled-for murder?" A D.C. local, J. G. Butler of St. Paul's Lutheran Church, called Lincoln the country's savior, proclaiming,

> He lives where the martyred men of all ages live—we believe, where the Great Martyr, our Lord Jesus, lives—in that heavenly City, whose air is not pregnant with treason and malice and death; but, where the heart, cleansed and inspired by the blood and spirit of Jesus, is in perfect and eternal sympathy with the great Redeemer, whose name is *love*.

A controversial politician widely blamed for the casualties and hardships of war, Lincoln was suddenly and forever upgraded to the persecuted savior who died so that the country might live.

A poster advertising the sunrise service stops me cold. It assumes, "You've seen *The Passion of the Christ.* Now celebrate the resurrection of the Christ."

I do enjoy a good movie tie-in. Plus, an event in the nation's capital rejoicing in the holy trinity of Jesus, Abraham Lincoln, and Mel Gibson witnessed on four hours of sleep—count me in.

The next morning, the Capitol dome is lit up white against the still black sky. I'm at the Lincoln Memorial by ten past six to strategize my seat location. Am I paranoid, or does the Easter service's powerful combination of a major Christian religious holiday celebrated on the National Mall in a patriotic shrine at the deep fond center of the American heart make the event the perfect target for a terrorist truck bomb? Before I left my hotel room, I e-mailed a friend where I was and where I was going and that if he saw an explosion at the Lincoln Memorial on the news he should phone my parents and break it to them I'm probably dead. I added a halfhearted "ha ha" at the end of the e-mail in an effort to fake breeziness, but truth is, I'm nervous.

As I stand before the front row of seats making a threat assessment, I rule out sitting in the folding chairs closest to the bandstand; it's fine if these born-again musicians want to call themselves the Resurrection Orchestra, but us nonbelievers flying without the net of an afterlife will be avoiding the blast radius of center stage.

Then, as if getting blown up is not enough to worry about, after I take a seat on the steps, I get a look at the choir. Thirty singers and from where I'm sitting it looks like only two of them are black. It's not like I'm saying suburban white people shouldn't sing. Because I love Van Halen's "Hot for Teacher." But as I suspected, at six-thirty sharp the choir does stand up to perform the first of their competent renditions of generic, mid-tempo pop ballads that sound like they were written by a computer using a database of Easter vocabulary. In fairness, I should mention that other people here love the choir. The crowd is clapping and swaying and raising their arms. For me, however, where gospel music is concerned, my taste is more conservative and narrowminded than a Reverend Falwell commencement address at Oral Roberts U. Unless it's an old holy-roller hymn Johnny Cash would have learned from his mama back in Arkansas, I'm not interested. So the only musical selection I sing along with is when the preacher, Amos Dodge, does a Martin Luther King and climbs halfway up the steps to lead us in an old-school, a cappella "How Great Thou Art."

Before delivering his sermon cum Mel Gibson movie review, the folksy Reverend Dodge intones, "As the old southern preacher said, 'If I don't light your fire, your wood's wet.' " It goes without saying that my wood is soggier than a sunken stump at the bottom of the Potomac. Still, I can't help but like this guy.

"Everybody's talking about *The Passion of the Christ*," he says. "I left the movie with my heart pierced. My steps were slow. I wanted to remember every scene, remember what I felt when I saw the whip, the soldiers, and the blood. But today we have come to celebrate the resurrection of the Christ from the dead.

"No other religion in the world has a risen savior," he brags, imagining that if the tombs of all the other historical religious figureheads were lined up "in a row at Arlington Cemetery across the river, they would all have 'Occupied' and 'No Vacancy' signs on the tombs, save one." I know Dodge doesn't intend for this to be a laugh line, but I crack up imagining one of the incarnations of the Buddha gunning down Nazis in World War II. "Only Jesus's tomb," continues Dodge, "would stand open and empty."

Here I've been under the impression that every time I come here to the Lincoln Memorial, I'm cheating death. Because the whole time I stand around reading his speeches, searching his eyes, I feel like I'm bringing Abraham Lincoln back to life.

Pastor Dodge brags that because of the story it tells, *The Passion of the Christ* is so popular that it is currently the eighth-largest-grossing movie of all time. I look around me at all the heads bowed in prayer, praying to this god they think or hope rose from the dead two thousand years ago just so he could offer them—us—everlasting life. Even I can see how, in terms of cheating death, the Christians' promise of everlasting life pretty much beats my staring-at-statues, reading-speeches-on-the-marble-wall method all to hell.

The service ends and I sit there on the steps for a while with "How Great Thou Art" stuck in my head. Elvis sang it, and I keep picturing the blue cover of his gospel album. It's one of my mother's favorites. She liked to put it on at Easter. She still does. For all I know, she was listening to Elvis's rendition of "How Great Thou Art" at the very moment I was warbling it here on the steps of the Lincoln Memorial.

Come to think of it, I can probably trace this whole morbid assassination death trip back to my parents' record collection. Specifically, Buddy Starcher's spoken-word LP *History Repeats Itself.* The title track hit number two on the pop charts back in 1966. When my sister and I were little, we used to scare ourselves by putting it on the record player and listening to Starcher rattle off a list of the spooky similarities between the Lincoln and Kennedy assassinations in a twangy accent while backup singers hum "The Battle Hymn of the Republic" underneath him as he talks.

Starcher's inventory includes the important facts that Lincoln was elected in 1860 and Kennedy in 1960; that both their vice presidents were named Johnson, the first Johnson being born in 1808 and the second one in 1908; that John Wilkes Booth was born in 1839 and Lee Harvey Oswald in 1939; that the names Lincoln and Kennedy each have seven letters, the names Andrew Johnson and Lyndon Johnson are thirteen letters each, and there are fifteen letters in the names John Wilkes Booth and Lee Harvey Oswald. Starcher concludes, "Friends, that these things are verified facts prove that truth really is stranger than fiction and that history *does* repeat itself."

Though Buddy Starcher has been forgotten, that list will never go away. Ann Landers seemed to get a column out of it every couple of years, most of which are easily found by typing the words "Landers" and "eerie" into a search engine. The Sixth Floor Museum in Dallas, which presents exhibits about the JFK assassination on the floor of the building where Oswald fired his rifle, sells it as a poster in the gift shop with pictures of the two presidents labeled "Lincoln-Kennedy Coincidence?"

While the list points out the fact that both presidential wives witnessed their husbands' murders and had children who died while their husbands were in the White House, the list daintily ignores the fact that both women spent way too much money on clothes. And then there is the ridiculous detail about how Booth shot Lincoln in a theater and then escaped to a warehouse, while Oswald shot Kennedy from a warehouse and then made haste to a theater. But Booth didn't run to a warehouse. He ended up in a barn. A barn is the same thing as a warehouse if you think that a puppet is the same thing as a potholder.

Still, as a kid, *History Repeats Itself* terrified me, mostly because I was a God-fearing child. And I mean that literally. God scared me stiff, what with the turning human beings into salt and getting them swallowed up by whales, plus the locusts and famines and, not least, making sure his own kid gets nailed to death onto wood. Every time someone would die—a cousin or grandparent or Elvis—some relative or preacher would there-there it away by saying that God has a plan, and we simply have no way of knowing what that plan is. But we did know. We learned about His plan every week at Sunday school. It's called Armageddon!

I think I saw the Kennedy-Lincoln coincidences as minor rest stops on the interstate to doomsday. I actually pictured God sitting on a cloud chuckling as He imagined blowing our miniature minds by making sure Oswald's mom got knocked up in time for her 1939 due date.

I no longer believe in a Supreme Being in the sky producing cosmic episodes of *Presidential Punk'd*. So why does that Kennedy-Lincoln list still spark something inside me? Why do I detect butterflies in my stomach every morning noticing how the headlines seem ripped from the McKinley administration? Or get the chills about the heap of peculiarity surrounding John Wilkes Booth's brother and Abraham Lincoln's son—Edwin Booth picking up Lincoln's plaster hands at that party, Edwin saving Robert Todd Lincoln's life, Ford's Theatre collapsing during Edwin's funeral, and of course the seriously hexed Robert T.'s assassination cameo three-peat?

Well, cue the "Battle Hymn" hummers. Because as Buddy Starcher would drawl, Friends, these creepy historical flukes offer momentary relief from the oppression of chaos and that is not nothing. They give order to the universe. They give meaning. Of course, life is still pretty meaningless and death is the only true democracy. But Robert Todd Lincoln, huh? *Weird.*

Time to go home. I walk down the steps of the Lincoln Memorial toward my uncle, then past the White House and the Seward plaque and on to Union Station and the train. Then to New York and my dead neighbors. From Penn Station to Madison Square Park to say hello to Chester Arthur. On to Gramercy Park to squint at fenced-in Edwin Booth, past Theodore Roosevelt's birthplace on Twentieth Street to Union Square, where Roosevelt's grandfather used to own a house, where as a boy Roosevelt sat in the window watching Abraham Lincoln's funeral cortege go by, where Emma Goldman gave a speech telling the parents of starving children to steal bread to feed them, where Henry Bacon, who built a Greek temple to Lincoln, built a bank, a Greek temple to money. Finally, turning toward home, I wave good-bye to Lincoln, whose bronze statue stands in the dead center of the square. Then I nod at Gandhi, whose bronze statue stands on the square's western edge. They shot him too.

ACKNOWLEDGMENTS

I cannot imagine writing a book without Geoffrey Kloske editing it to the point that I have begun to fear his death more than my own. Though I don't know how I can keep my head from getting too big thanks to constant fawning praise from Geoff like, "I guess that idea isn't *too* terrible." I'm also cheerfully indebted to David Rosenthal, Rachel Nagler, Caroline Bruce, Laura Perciasepe, and Christopher Wahlers at Simon & Schuster; Karen Covington and Byrd Schas for transcribing tapes; Marcel Dzama for his illustrations; and once again, David Levinthal for his cover photograph.

Also propping me up: Jaime Wolf, Esquire; Kathie Russo, and Jaime Askin at Washington Square Arts; Kathryn Barcos, Eliza Fischer, and it goes without saying Steven "the Colonel" Barclay of the Steven Barclay Agency.

Thanks always and especially to: my parents, Pat and Janie Vowell; Greil and Jenny Marcus; David Rakoff, Dave Eggers, and Ira Glass, whose editorial mojo is so potent all I have to do is imagine him reading some dull and long-winded passage that I dutifully cut it down to a pithier point without being told.

As well as: Kevin Baker, Alex Blumberg, Eric Bogosian, Shelley Dick, Daniel Ferguson, John Flansburgh, Barrett Golding, Jonathan Goldstein, Robin Goldwasser, Jack Hitt,

John Hodgman, Nick Hornby, Ben Karlin, Jon Langford, Lisa Leingang, Ben Lloyd, John Ma, Jim Nelson, Conan O'Brien, Kate Porterfield, David Sedaris, John-Mario Sevilla, Jeff Singer, Julie Snyder, the Family Sontheimer, Wendy Weil, and Ren Weschler. A welcome distraction from assassination conspiracies were these conspiracies I'm thrilled to be part of: *This American Life, McSweeney's,* Pixar, Eating It, *Late Night,* the New York Institute for the Humanities at NYU, and 826NYC.

A special Shotgun! to my fellow travelers: my sister Amy Vowell; my nephew Owen Brooker; Fran and Quenton Barker; Nicole Francis; Brent Hoff; Matt Klam; Matt Roberts; and particularly the Lincoln-loving Bennett Miller, who is either a really good listener or a really good actor—he's been this book's best friend.

As this book was going to press, I was dismayed to learn of Gretchen Worden's death. The director of Philadelphia's Mütter Museum, she was only fifty-six. The world is a little less interesting without her in it.

ABOUT THE AUTHOR

SARAH VOWELL is the author of *The Wordy Shipmates*, *Assassination Vacation*, *The Partly Cloudy Patriot*, *Take the Cannoli*, and *Radio On*. A contributing editor for public radio's *This American Life*, she lives in New York City.

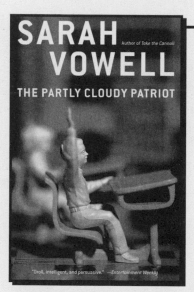
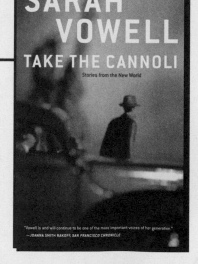
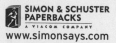